MW00987333

THE
BIG BOOK
OF
STATE
FACTS

THE
BIG BOOK
OF
STATE
FACTS

Over 2,600 Facts of American
History Separated by State!

O. MICHAEL MAYSAM

Boundary Peak Publishing
Las Vegas, Nevada

Copyright © 2023 by O. Michael Maysam

ALL RIGHTS RESERVED

No portion of this book may be reproduced without written permission from the publisher or author except as permitted by U.S. copyright law.

Every reasonable effort has been made to trace copyright holders of material reproduced in this book, but if any have inadvertently overlooked, the publisher would be glad to hear from them.

Paperback ISBN: 979-8-9891977-0-5
Hardcover ISBN: 979-8-9891977-1-2
eBook ISBN: 979-8-9891977-2-9
Large Print Paperback ISBN: 979-8-9891977-3-6

10 9 8 7 6 5 4 3 2 1

First Edition

To explore our full collection of titles and stay up to date with Boundary Peak Publishing news, please visit us at https://www.boundarypeakpub.com/ or scan the QR code below to be taken to our website.

If you have enjoyed this book, please leave us a review on Amazon or on the platform where you purchased this book from.

Follow us on YouTube and TikTok for more exciting facts!

YouTube: https://www.youtube.com/@BoundaryPeak
TikTok: https://www.tiktok.com/@boundarypeak

The world is a book and those who do not travel read only one page.

—Saint Augustine

For those with a passion for learning.

CONTENTS

INTRODUCTION

Welcome to "The Big Book of State Facts," your in-depth resource for learning about the richly varied and intriguing fabric of the United States of America. The following pages will take you on a fantastic journey across all 50 states, Washington, D.C., and more, revealing more than 2,600 fascinating and educational facts along the way.

The United States has extraordinary diversity, from the soaring Rockies to the sun-drenched beaches of Florida, the pulsating city of New York to the quiet serenity of Montana's wildness. With a rich tapestry of history, culture, geography, and trivia, each state adds its distinct flavor to the American mosaic, making this country truly distinctive.

"The Big Book of State Facts" is your passport to explore the hidden gems, untold stories, and captivating details that define each state's identity. Whether you're a lifelong resident, a curious traveler, a student, or simply someone with a thirst for knowledge, this book promises to delight and inform you.

You're bound to find the well-known facts and the lesser-known treasures that make every state special. From famous landmarks and historical events to quirky traditions and natural wonders, I've gathered an impressive array of facts to satisfy your curiosity about the land you call home or dream of visiting.

Whether you're looking for fascinating trivia to share at your next gathering, aiming to expand your knowledge of the United States, training for Jeopardy, preparing for the next trivia night, or seeking inspiration for your next adventure, "The Big Book of State Facts" is your go-to resource. Join us on this immersive journey through America's rich and diverse tapestry, and prepare to be amazed, informed, and entertained as you discover the countless wonders that make each state unique. Enjoy your exploration!

ALABAMA

1. Alabama is known as the "Heart of Dixie," the "Yellowhammer State," and the "Cotton State."

2. Alaska was the 22nd state admitted to the Union on December 14, 1819.

3. Alabama's state motto is "Audemus jura nostra defendere," which means "We dare defend our rights.

4. Mobile, Alabama, is believed to have had the first Mardi Gras celebration in the United States in 1703, even before New Orleans.

5. Helen Keller, a famous author and political activist who was both blind and deaf, was born in Tuscumbia, Alabama.

6. The state has a rich history related to the civil rights movement, with significant events occurring in places like Montgomery and Birmingham.

7. Alabama is home to the U.S. Space & Rocket Center in Huntsville, which features the Saturn V rocket that sent astronauts to the moon.

8. The town of Enterprise is known for its Boll Weevil Monument, erected to recognize the insect's unintentional positive impact on the local economy.

9. The Edmund Pettus Bridge in Selma played a significant role in the civil rights movement and was the site of the infamous "Bloody Sunday" incident.

10. The world's first electric trolly system was introduced in Montgomery, Alabama, in 1886.

11. Alabama was a major cotton producer during the 19th century, leading to the nickname "Cotton State."

12. Muscle Shoals is known for its influential music scene, with recording studios attracting artists like Aretha Franklin and the Rolling Stones.

13. The Confederate flag was designed in Marion, Alabama, in 1861 and became the symbol of the Confederate States of America.

14. Alabama's state constitution comprises approximately 389,000 words, making it the longest state governing document in the United States.

15. Alabama is home to the Talladega Superspeedway, one of the fastest tracks in NASCAR racing.

16. Birmingham has a unique "Vulcan" statue, the largest cast iron statue in the world.

17. Alabama's official state nut is the pecan.

18. The Conecuh Ridge Distillery in Alabama produced the iconic American whiskey called Clyde May's Alabama-style whiskey.

19. The USS Alabama battleship, now a museum in Mobile, served during World War II.

20. The town of Aliceville hosts the Aliceville Museum, dedicated to preserving the history of the German prisoners of war held there during World War II.

21. The town of Prattville has the Cross Garden, known for its numerous crosses and biblical messages displayed throughout the property.

22. The state's official state mineral is hematite.

23. Magnolia Springs, Alabama, has the only U.S. Postal Service route where a boat is used to deliver mail.

24. The city of Florence is the birthplace of W.C. Handy, often called the "Father of the Blues."

25. Alabama's Gulf Coast is a popular vacation destination with beautiful beaches.

26. The state hosts the National Shrimp Festival in Gulf Shores, Alabama.

27. The Freedom Rides Museum in Montgomery commemorates the efforts of civil rights activists who challenged segregation on interstate buses.

28. The Hodges Meteorite, a space rock that fell in 1954, is famous for being the only meteorite to have struck a human.

29. Alabama's Conecuh Sausage Company in Evergreen, Alabama, produces a well-known variety of smoked sausage.

30. The Coon Dog Cemetery in Cherokee is a unique burial ground exclusively for coonhounds, complete with headstones and memorabilia.

31. The Tuskegee Airman, a group of African-American fighter and bomber pilots who fought during World War II, were trained at the Tuskegee Institute. The Tuskegee Institute is now known as Tuskegee University and is located near Tuskegee, Alabama.

32. Mobile is known for its Azalea Trail Maids, a group of young women who serve as cultural ambassadors for the city during events.

33. The Mobile Carnival Museum celebrates the history and artistry of Mardi Gras in Mobile.

34. The state has several mysterious and unexplained landmarks, such as the "Face in the Courthouse Window" in Carrollton.

35. The Old Cahawba Archaeological Park preserves the remnants of a former state capital that was abandoned in the 19th century.

36. The town of Monroeville was the inspiration for the fictional Maycomb in Harper Lee's classic novel "To Kill a Mockingbird."

37. Alabama is known for its delicious Southern cuisine, including fried chicken, collard greens, and biscuits.

38. Mary Anderson created windshield wipers in Green County, Alabama, and filed a patent for the invention in 1903.

39. The city of Gadsden is the start of the World's Longest Yard Sale, an annual event stretching over 690 miles, ending in Addison, Michigan.

40. The Civil Rights Memorial in Montgomery honors those who died during the struggle for civil rights.

41. Alabama's state amphibian is the Red Hills salamander.

42. The city of Huntsville hosts the annual "Big Spring Jam," a music festival featuring a diverse range of artists.

43. The state's official state fossil is the *Basilosaurus,* an ancient whale species.

45. Alabama's state dance is the square dance.

46. The Hank Williams Museum in Montgomery commemorates the iconic country music singer.

47. The Alabama Museum of Natural History in Tuscaloosa features exhibits on geology, paleontology, and native wildlife.

48. Alabama's state crustacean is the brown shrimp.

49. The state's official insect is the Monarch butterfly.

50. The town of Eufaula is known for its annual "Eufaula Pilgrimage," showcasing historic homes and architecture.

ALASKA

1. Alaska is the largest state in the United States, covering an area of over 663,000 square miles.

2. Alaska is the least densely populated state, with only around 1.2 people per square mile.

3. Alaska was purchased from Russia for $7.2 million in 1867 (the equivalent of $148.7 million in 2023), a deal known as the "Alaska Purchase" of "Seward's Folly."

4. The state's official nickname is "The Last Frontier."

5. The Alaska Highway, also known as the Alcan Highway, was built during World War II to connect Alaska to the rest of the United States through Canada.

6. The highest point in North America, Denali (formerly known as Mount McKinley), is in Alaska, reaching 20,310 feet (6,194 meters).

7. Alaska has more coastline than the rest of the United States combined.

8. The state is home to over 100,000 glaciers, including the famous Mendenhall Glacier near Juneau.

9. Juneau, the capital of Alaska, is the only U.S. capital that is not accessible by road; it's only accessible by boat or plane.

10. Alaska has the longest daylight hours during its summer months, with some areas experiencing nearly 24 hours of daylight.

11. The Northern Lights, or Aurora Borealis, are a common sight in Alaska due to their location near the North Pole.

12. The Aleutian Islands, a chain of volcanic islands, stretch across the Bering Sea and connect Alaska to Russia.

13. The state is home to diverse wildlife, including bears (grizzly and black bears), moose, caribou, wolves, and bald eagles.

14. Alaska has more than three million lakes, making it an ideal destination for fishing and outdoor activities. Of the three million lakes, only around 3,200 are officially named.

15. The official state bird of Alaska is the Willow Ptarmigan, a type of grouse that changes color with the seasons.

16. The Iditarod Trail Sled Dog Race, known as the "Last Great Race on Earth," covers over 1,000 miles of challenging terrain from Anchorage to Nome.

17. Alaska's economy relies heavily on oil and natural gas production, with the Trans-Alaska Pipeline System transporting oil from Prudhoe Bay to Valdez.

18. Kodiak Island is home to the Kodiak bear, one of the largest species of bears in the world.

19. The city of Barrow, Alaska, experiences polar nights during winter, where the sun does not rise for several weeks.

20. The city of Sitka was the capital of Russian America before it was sold to the United States.

21. Alaska has 12 of the 20 highest peaks in the United States.

22. The state has various Native cultures, including the Iñupiat, Eskimo, Aleut, and Tlingit peoples.

23. Alaska is known for its world-class fishing, including salmon, halibut, and trout.

24. The Alaska Marine Highway System operates a network of ferry routes connecting many coastal communities.

25. Anchorage, the largest city in Alaska, contains over 40 percent of the state's population.

26. The Hubbard Glacier in Alaska is one of North America's most active and fastest-moving glaciers.

27. The state's diverse ecosystems range from rainforests in the southern to tundra in the north and west.

28. Alaska has more active volcanoes than any other state, including Mount Redoubt, Mount Augustine, and Mount Spurr.

29. The Yukon River is the third-longest river in the United States and flows through interior Alaska.

30. The state has a strong indigenous art scene, with traditional crafts such as basketry, carving, and beadwork.

31. Alaska's state flag was designed by a 14-year-old Native Alaskan boy named Benny Benson in 1927.

32. The town of Whittier has a unique arrangement where most residents live in the same building due to the harsh climate and terrain.

33. Alaska has a state sport: dog mushing, which is the use of sled dogs to transport people and goods.

34. The Midnight Sun Baseball Game is an annual event held in Fairbanks, where a baseball game is played without artificial lighting during the summer solstice.

35. Alaska's vast wilderness offers opportunities for adventure activities like hiking, kayaking, and backcountry skiing.

36. The Alaska State Fair holds the Giant Cabbage Weigh-Off, where enormous cabbages can weigh over 100 pounds.

37. The state has over 1,000 named islands and thousands of unnamed ones.

38. The Alaska Native Claims Settlement Act of 1971 settled land claims with indigenous groups and created regional Native corporations.

39. Alaska was home to the Klondike Gold Rush, and the town of Skagway still retains a historic feel thanks to it.

40. The official state flower of Alaska is the forget-me-not.

41. There are more than 12,000 rivers in Alaska.

42. Alaska's glaciers store more water than anywhere outside of Greenland and Antarctica.

43. The Aleut language has one of the smallest speaker populations, making it endangered.

44. Alaskans celebrate "Fur Rondy," a winter festival with events like the Running of the Reindeer and fur auctions.

45. The city of Nome is famous for the annual Iditarod Trail Sled Dog Race finish and its history related to the Gold Rush.

46. Alaska's state gem is jade, and the state is known for its rich deposits of this precious stone.

47. The Alaska Railroad offers scenic train rides through some of the state's most stunning landscapes.

48. The Alaska State Museum in Juneau showcases the state's rich cultural heritage and history.

49. The state's diverse marine life includes whales, sea lions, otters, and numerous fish species.

50. Alaska's rugged terrain and challenging weather have made it a destination for outdoor enthusiasts seeking extreme adventures.

ARIZONA

1. Arizona is known as the "Grand Canyon State.

2. It became the 48th state to join the Union on February 14, 1912.

3. Another one of Arizona's nicknames, "The Copper State," reflects its history of copper mining.

4. Arizona's capital is Phoenix, the fifth most populous city in the United States.

5. The Grand Canyon, in northern Arizona, is one of the Seven Natural Wonders of the World.

6. The state's official flower is the saguaro cactus blossom.

7. Arizona's official state bird is the cactus wren.

8. The Barringer Meteor Crater near Winslow is one of the best-preserved impact craters on Earth.

9. The Petrified Forest National Park contains fossilized trees that lived over 225 million years ago.

10. The world's largest rose bush, known as the "Lady Banksia Rose," can be found in Tombstone, Arizona. The bush covers around 9,000 square feet (836 square meters).

11. The town of Oatman is known for its wild burros that roam freely on the streets.

12. The Arizona-Sonora Desert Museum in Tucson showcases the region's diverse desert flora and fauna.

13. The London Bridge, originally spanning the River Thames in London, was transported and reassembled in Lake Havasu City, Arizona.

14. The city of Flagstaff is one of the best places in the U.S. to view the stars due to its dark skies and high elevation.

15. Jerome is often called the "Largest Ghost Town in America" and is known for its artistic community.

16. The Painted Desert in northeastern Arizona is known for its colorful and breathtaking landscape.

17. The McMath-Pierce Solar Telescope, located at Kitt Peak National Observatory, was once the largest solar telescope in the world.

18. Sedona is famous for its stunning red rock formations and New Age spirituality culture.

19. The Four Corners Monument is the only point in the United States where four states (Arizona, Colorado, New Mexico, and Utah) meet.

20. The deserts in Arizona are the wettest in the world, averaging between 4.7 and up to 11.8 inches of rain annually.

21. The Hoover Dam, on the Arizona-Nevada border, was constructed during the Great Depression and is a marvel of engineering.

22. Biosphere 2 is an experimental ecological facility located near Tucson and was designed to replicate Earth's ecosystems.

23. Arizona's Organ Pipe Cactus National Monument is home to the rare organ pipe cactus.

24. The world's oldest rodeo, the Prescott Frontier Days Rodeo, takes place annually in Prescott and started in 1888.

25. The town of Patagonia is known for its vibrant arts scene and unique shops.

26. The "Apache Trail" is a scenic drive through the Superstition Mountains and offers stunning views.

27. The Tonto National Monument contains well-preserved cliff dwellings built by ancient indigenous peoples.

28. Arizona's Kartchner Caverns State Park features "Big Room," one of the world's largest cave rooms.

29. The Lowell Observatory in Flagstaff is where Pluto was discovered in 1930.

30. Arizona's state fish is the Apache trout.

31. The state's official state reptile is the Arizona ridge-nosed rattlesnake.

32. The Biosphere 2 facility was used for scientific experiments in the early 1990s to study self-sustaining ecosystems.

33. Bisbee is famous for its historic mining district and colorful architecture.

34. Monument Valley, located on the Arizona-Utah border, has been featured in numerous films and TV shows.

35. The Saguaro National Park protects the iconic saguaro cactus, which can grow up to 70 feet tall.

36. Arizona gave women the right to vote eight years before national suffrage was enacted.

37. The Titan Missile Museum near Tucson offers tours of a former intercontinental ballistic missile silo.

38. The "Skywalk" at the Grand Canyon West allows visitors to walk on a glass platform extending over the canyon's edge.

39. The state's official fossil is the petrified wood from the Araucarioxylon arizonicum tree.

40. The Arizona-Sonora Desert Museum combines a zoo, botanical garden, and natural history museum.

41. The Turquoise Room at La Posada Hotel in Winslow is known for its gourmet Native American cuisine.

42. The Heard Museum in Phoenix showcases Native American art and culture.

43. Kartchner Caverns was kept secret for over 14 years to protect its delicate formations from vandalism.

44. A citywide UFO sighting transpired in Phoenix, Arizona, in 1997.

45. The rocks in the Grand Canyon are older than dinosaurs.

46. The town of Yuma is the "Sunniest City on Earth," with over 4,000 hours of sunshine per year.

47. The city of Scottsdale is famous for its luxurious resorts, golf courses, and spa facilities.

48. The Navajo Nation is the largest Native American-held land in the United States. The majority is within the borders of Arizona and is over 17.5 million acres (70,000 square kilometers) in size. If the area were considered a state, it would be the 11th largest.

49. The U.S. Postal Service used mules to deliver mail to the Havasupai, a group of Native Americans who live at the bottom of the Grand Canyon.

50. Arizona is home to the Gila Monster, one of two venomous lizards in the world and the only one in America.

ARKANSAS

1. Arkansas is known as the "Natural State."

2. It became the 25th state to join the Union on June 15, 1836.

3. The state's capital is Little Rock.

4. The Ozark Mountains cover a significant portion of northern Arkansas.

5. Hot Springs National Park is home to natural hot springs that Native Americans used for their therapeutic properties.

6. Arkansas is home to the only active diamond mine in the United States, the Crater of Diamonds State Park.

7. The state's official gemstone is the diamond.

8. The Buffalo National River is the first designated National River in the United States.

9. The *King Biscuit Time* radio show in Helena is one of history's longest-running daily radio broadcasts.

10. The town of Eureka Springs is known for its Victorian architecture and unique cultural scene.

11. Arkansas is known for its distinct style of barbecue, characterized by its emphasis on pork and tangy vinegar-based sauces.

12. The city of Fayetteville hosts the annual Bikes, Blues & BBQ motorcycle rally.

13. The Johnny Cash Music Festival is held annually in Jonesboro to honor the legendary musician.

14. The town of Hope is the birthplace of former President Bill Clinton.

15. Arkansas's official state insect is the honeybee.

16. The state's official state bird is the northern mockingbird.

17. Mount Ida is called the Quartz "Crystal Capital of the World."

18. The city of Fort Smith was a prominent frontier outpost during the Wild West era.

19. The American Taekwondo Association's national headquarters is in Little Rock.

20. The Ouachita National Forest has more than 700 types of trees and shrubs.

21. The Daisy Airgun Museum in Rogers showcases the history of the famous Daisy BB guns.

22. The Little Rock Central High School National Historic Site commemorates the desegregation crisis in 1957.

23. The town of Alma hosts the annual Spinach Festival, celebrating its history as a spinach-growing area.

24. The World's Championship Duck Calling Contest is held annually in Stuttgart.

25. The William J. Clinton Presidential Library and Museum is in Little Rock.

26. The state's official state beverage is milk.

27. Arkansas was originally part of the Union during the Civil War. It joined the Confederacy in May of 1861.

28. The town of Gillett hosts the annual Gillett Coon Supper, a tradition since 1933. The main dish of the supper is raccoon, and thousands of pounds of meat are served each year.

29. The first documentation of "cheese dip" was in Hot Springs, Arkansas, in 1935 at the Mexico Chiquito restaurant.

30. Arkansas is known for its diverse natural beauty, including rivers, lakes, forests, and mountains.

31. The Arkansas River is the sixth-longest river in the United States.

32. Arkansas's state soil is the Stuttgart soil series.

33. Magnolia is home to the World's Largest Charcoal Grill.

34. Hattie Caraway, the first elected woman senator, was elected from Arkansas in 1932.

35. The city of Bentonville is home to the Crystal Bridges Museum of American Art, showcasing a unique collection of American artworks.

36. Arkansas's official state dinosaur is the Arkansaurus fridayi.

37. The town of Mountain View is famous for its Ozark Folk Festival and traditional music scene.

38. The state's official fruit is the South Arkansas vine ripe pink tomato.

39. Arkansas has diverse wildlife, including black bears, bobcats, and alligators.

40. The Arkansas Alligator Farm and Petting Zoo in Hot Springs allows visitors to see alligators up close.

41. The town of Dumas hosts the annual Ding Dong Days festival, named after a historic doorbell factory.

42. The Big Dam Bridge in Little Rock is the longest pedestrian and bicycle bridge in the United States.

43. Arkansas's official state flower is the apple blossom.

44. Mammoth Spring in Mammoth Spring, Arkansas, is one of the largest natural springs in the world.

45. The annual World Championship Cardboard Boat Races are held in Heber Springs.

46. Arkansas has more than 40 natural springs throughout the state.

47. The Hemingway-Pfeiffer Museum in Piggot was once the home of author Ernest Hemingway's second wife's family.

48. The Delta Cultural Center in Helena showcases the culture and history   of the Mississippi Delta region in Arkansas.

49. Dillard's department stores started from a single location in Mineral Springs, Arkansas, in 1938.

50. More than half of Arkansas is covered by forestland.

CALIFORNIA

1. California is the most populous state in the United States, surpassing Texas by almost nine million more people.

2. California became the 31st state to join the Union on September 9, 1850.

3. California's nickname is the "Golden State."

4. The state's capital is Sacramento.

5. The iconic Golden Gate Bridge, located in San Francisco, is one of the most photographed bridges in the world.

6. California is known for its diverse landscapes, including beaches, deserts, forests, and mountains.

7. The state's official state flower is the California poppy.

8. The world's tallest tree, Hyperion, a coast redwood, is in Redwood National Park, measuring 380 feet (115.92 meters) tall.

9. California is home to Silicon Valley, the global technology and innovation center.

10. The state's official state bird is the California quail.

11. Hollywood, located in Los Angeles, is known as the world's entertainment capital and is home to the U.S. film industry.

12. The Hollywood Walk of Fame features over 2,700 brass stars in the sidewalk to honor notable personalities.

13. California produces more than 80% of all the wine in the United States.

14. The state's official land animal is the California grizzly bear.

15. Yosemite National Park is renowned for its stunning granite cliffs, waterfalls, and ancient sequoia trees.

16. Death Valley, located in Eastern California, is the hottest and driest national park in the U.S. On July 10, 1913, the temperature reached 134 degrees Fahrenheit (56.67 degrees Celsius).

17. California is the third-largest state by land area.

18. The state's official freshwater fish is the California golden trout.

19. The city of Los Angeles is home to the Getty Center, an art museum known for its impressive architecture and art collections.

20. Lake Tahoe, situated in the Sierra Nevada Mountains, forming a border with Nevada, is the largest alpine lake in North America.

21. The California State Railroad Museum in Sacramento showcases the history of rail transportation in the state.

22. California is known for its vibrant surf culture, with world-famous surf spots along the coast.

23. The original name of California was *Las Californias*, a name given to the state by the Spaniards. The name was the name of the mythical island, "California," in a 1510 fiction novel, *The Adventures of Esplandián*, by Garci Rodríguez de Montalvo.

24. Joshua Tree National Park features unique desert landscapes and iconic Joshua trees.

25. California is home to the highest peak in the contiguous United States, Mount Whitney.

26. The San Andreas Fault, a major tectonic boundary, runs through California and is responsible for earthquakes in the region.

27. A total of 15 Major League Baseball (MLB), National Basketball Association (NBA), National Football League (NFL), and National Hockey League (NHL) call California home—more than any other state. Florida has the next highest number at nine. California is also home to three Major League Soccer (MLS) teams.

28. The California Science Center in Los Angeles houses the Space Shuttle *Endeavor*.

29. California is home to many world-class universities, including Stanford University and the University of California system.

30. California's diverse agricultural industry produces various crops, including fruits, vegetables, and nuts.

31. Disneyland, located in Anaheim, was the first-ever theme park built by Walt Disney. The park opened in 1955.

32. California is the only state to have hosted both the Summer and Winter Olympic Games.

33. The Monterey Bay Aquarium is known for its marine exhibits and conservation efforts.

34. The San Francisco Cable Cars are the world's last manually operated cable car system.

35. The California Academy of Sciences in San Francisco is one of the largest natural history museums in the world.

36. Alcatraz Island, located in San Francisco Bay, was once home to a notorious federal prison.

37. California's coastline stretches over 800 miles along the Pacific Ocean.

38. Sequoia National Park is home to some of the world's largest trees, including the General Sherman Tree.

39. The California State Capitol in Sacramento is an architectural marvel and a historic site.

40. California is known for its progressive environmental policies and efforts to combat climate change.

41. The state's official state dance is the West Coast Swing.

42. The San Diego Zoo is among the world's largest and most famous.

43. California was its own country for a few weeks in 1846.

44. The full name of Los Angeles is "El Pueblo de Nuestra Señora la Reina de los Ángeles del Río Porciúncula," which translates to "The Town of Our Lady the Queen of Angels of the River Porciúncula."

45. California is home to the lowest (Badwater Basin - 282 feet below sea level) and the highest points (Mount Whitney - 14,505 feet above sea level) in the continental United States.

46. At one point, walking down the streets in San Francisco was illegal if you were classified as "ugly."

47. Los Angeles County has over 5,000 oil and gas wells hidden in residential neighborhoods and commercial areas.

48. California has nine national parks, more than any other state.

49. From 1981 to 1994, a dog was the elected mayor of Sunol, California, defeating two human candidates for the position. The dog's name was Bosco Ramos.

50. Half of the United States' fruits and vegetables and two-thirds of the United States' fruits and nuts come from California.

COLORADO

1. Colorado is known as the "Centennial State" because it became a state in 1876, exactly 100 years after the signing of the Declaration of Independence.

2. The state's capital is Denver, also known as the "Mile-High City" due to its elevation of exactly one mile (5,280 feet) above sea level.

3. Colorado is home to the Rocky Mountains, including the famous peaks of Pikes Peak and Longs Peak.

4. The highest point in the state is Mount Elbert, which reaches 14,440 feet (4,401 meters).

5. Mesa Verde National Park contains some of the best-preserved Native American cliff dwellings in the United States.

6. Colorado is the only state in history to decline to host the Olympics. Denver was awarded the 1976 Winter Olympics but later declined due to financial concerns.

7. The state's official flower is the Rocky Mountain columbine, known for its distinctive blue and white petals. It is illegal to pick the flower on public land or without prior consent of a private landowner.

8. Colorado is the eighth-largest state in terms of land area.

9. The Great Sand Dunes National Park features the tallest sand dunes in North America.

10. The state's official state tree is the Colorado blue spruce.

11. Denver International Airport is the largest airport in the Western Hemisphere by land area and the second largest on Earth.

12. Louis Ballast reportedly created the first cheeseburger in Denver in the late 1920s at the Humpty Dumpty Barrel restaurant.

13. The state is home to numerous craft breweries, contributing to its reputation as a hub for beer enthusiasts.

14. Garden of the Gods in Colorado Springs showcases stunning red rock formations and is a popular destination for outdoor enthusiasts.

15. Colorado's official state fish is the greenback cutthroat trout, which is native to the state.

16. The world's highest cog railway, The Broadmoor Manitou and Pikes Peak Cog Railway takes visitors to the summit of Pikes Peak, 14,110 feet above sea level.

17. Red Rocks Amphitheatre near Denver is a famous outdoor music venue with natural acoustics and stunning surroundings.

18. The first licensed African-American female physician in the United States, Dr. Justina Ford, practiced in Denver.

19. The Royal Gorge Bridge near Cañon City is one of the highest suspension bridges in the world, with a deck height of 955 feet measured from the deck to the river surface below. It is the highest bridge in the United States.

20. Colorado has diverse climate zones, ranging from arid deserts to alpine tundra.

21. The state's official state insect is the Colorado hairstreak butterfly.

22. The Colorado River, one of the major rivers in the western United States, flows through the state.

23. Alma, Colorado, at an elevation of 10,361 feet (3,158 meters), is the highest incorporated city in the United States.

24. The state hosts the annual Great American Beer Festival in Denver, Colorado, one of the largest beer festivals in the world.

25. Colorado was the first state to legalize recreational marijuana use for adults in 2012.

26. The Stanley Hotel in Estes Park inspired Steven King's novel *The Shining*.

27. The Denver Mint produces more than 50 million coins daily, making it one of the world's largest producers of coin currency.

28. Colorado Springs is home to the United States Olympic & Paralympic Committee Headquarters.

29. Colorado's Black Canyon of the Gunnison National Park features one of North America's steepest and narrowest canyons.

30. The Great Divide, marking the separation between the watersheds of the Pacific and Atlantic Oceans, runs through Colorado.

31. The state's official mammal is the Rocky Mountain bighorn sheep.

32. Telluride is famous for its film festival and stunning mountain scenery.

33. Colorado's Black Forest is home to the country's highest density of Ponderosa pine trees.

34. Colorado has the highest lowest point of any state. Sitting at 3,315 feet above sea level, the Arikaree River is the lowest point in the state.

35. The state's official state fossil is the stegosaurus.

36. The Colorado State Capitol in Denver is made of Colorado Rose Onyx, a rare stone.

37. The Durango & Silverton Narrow Gauge Railroad offers scenic rides through the San Juan Mountains.

38. Colorado Springs is home to the United States Air Force Academy.

39. Throwing snowballs at someone or a building is illegal in Aspen, Colorado, which is a popular winter resort town.

40. No President or Vice-President of The United States has been born in Colorado.

41. Fruita, Colorado, was home to "Mike the Headless Chicken." Mike had his head cut off and continued to live for another 18 months, eventually dying in 1947. In May, an annual "Mike the Headless Chicken Day" is held in Fruita.

42. Runway 16R/34L at Denver International Airport is 16,000 feet (3.03 miles; 4.88 kilometers) long, making it the seventh longest on Earth and the longest public-use runway in North America.

43. A concert violinist invented the "parking boot" in Denver, Colorado, in 1944. Frank Marugg created what was initially known as the "Denver Boot."

44. Colfax Avenue in Denver is the longest continuous street in the United States. The road runs for just over 50 miles.

45. Dove Creek, Colorado, is known as the "Pinto Bean Capital of the World."

46. Colorado is home to over 600 ghost towns.

47. The world's largest hot springs pool can be found in Glenwood Springs, Colorado, at Glenwood Hot Springs.

48. The 13th step of the State Capitol Building marks precisely one mile above sea level.

49. Denver, Colorado, has more than 300 parks.

50. Buckhorn Exchange in Denver was the first establishment to receive a liquor license in the state of Colorado after Prohibition.

CONNECTICUT

1. Connecticut is known as the "Constitution State" due to its early adoption of a state constitution in 1639. The constitution was known as the Fundamental Orders.

2. It was one of the original thirteen colonies and the fifth state to join the Union on January 9, 1788.

3. The state's capital is Hartford, while its largest city is Bridgeport.

4. Connecticut is famous for its picturesque coastal towns, making it a popular summer destination.

5. Yale University, one of the prestigious Ivy League Schools, is in New Haven, Connecticut.

6. The city of New London is home to the United States Coast Guard Academy.

7. The Connecticut River is the longest river in New England, flowing through the state's central region.

8. The Mark Twain House & Museum in Hartford was once the famous author's home.

9. The lollipop was invented in New Haven, Connecticut, in 1908.

10. In 1728, the first steel mill to operate in the United States was opened in Simsbury, Connecticut.

11. The Charter Oak, a famous white oak tree in Hartford, hid Connecticut's royal charter in 1687.

12. The state's official insect is the European mantis.

13. Connecticut was a significant center for the American clock and watch industry in the 19th century. The American Clock & Watch Museum in Bristol, Connecticut, is dedicated to horology.

14. The Foxwoods Resort Casino in Mashantucket is one of the largest casinos in the world.

15. The state's official state song is "Yankee Doodle."

16. Connecticut's official state bird is the American robin.

17. The first U.S. submarine, *Turtle*, was built in Connecticut during the American Revolution.

18. The Connecticut Wine Trail features numerous wineries and vineyards across the state.

19. Lake Compounce in Bristol is one of the oldest continuously operating amusement parks in the United States.

20. The Old State House in Hartford is one of the oldest state houses in the country.

21. Connecticut is part of the densely populated Tri-State Area region alongside New York and New Jersey.

22. The state has an official state hero, Nathan Hale, a Revolutionary War spy who famously said, "I only regret that I have but one life to lose for my country."

23. The first telephone exchange was established in New Haven, Connecticut, in 1878.

24. The state's official state ship is the USS Nautilus, the world's first nuclear-powered submarine.

25. Connecticut's official state animal is the sperm whale.

26. The world's first phone book was published in New Haven, Connecticut.

27. The Ivoryton Playhouse in Ivoryton is one of the oldest operating theaters in the United States.

28. The Weir Farm National Historic Site in Wilton is the only national park dedicated to American painting.

29. The first public library in the United States, the Scoville Memorial Library, was established in Salisbury, Connecticut, in 1803.

30. Connecticut gets its name from the Connecticut River.

31. The largest maritime museum in the United States is Mystic Seaport, located in Mystic, Connecticut.

32. Chester, Connecticut, is known for hosting an annual "rubber ducky race."

33. Connecticut is home to the oldest surviving state prison in the United States, the Old New-Gate Prison & Copper Mine, built in 1775.

34. Connecticut was the first state to impose a speed limit for automobiles. The speed limit was 15 miles per hour for rural roads and 12 miles per hour for city roads.

35. Connecticut is home to the inventor of the revolver, Samuel Colt.

36. The frisbee was invented in Connecticut by William Russell Frisbie.

37. The Wadsworth Atheneum Museum in Hartford is the oldest public art museum in the United States.

38. Connecticut is the fourth most densely populated state.

39. New Haven and Hartford were Connecticut's capitals at the same time from 1701 to 1874.

40. The Hartford Courant is the oldest continuously published newspaper in the United States.

41. The world's first helicopter's first practical flight was in Connecticut in 1939.

42. Lyme disease owes its name to the fact that it was first discovered in Lyme, Connecticut, in 1975.

43. Kissing your wife on Sundays in Connecticut used to be illegal.

44. The name Connecticut means "long tidal river."

45. The first written Constitution in the world was created in Connecticut in 1639. The Constitution was known as the Fundamental Orders.

46. Using a white walking cane in Connecticut is illegal unless you are blind.

47. Connecticut is home to the first woman to receive a U.S. Patent, Mary Kies of South Killingly, Connecticut.

48. The first accredited music school in the United States was opened in Salem, Connecticut. Music Vale Seminary was opened in 1835 by Orramel Whittlesey.

49. New Haven, Connecticut, is home to New Haven-style pizza, which has been voted the best in the world.

50. Connecticut is home to the oldest steam-powered cider mill in the United States. B.F. Clyde's Cider Mill is located in Mystic, Connecticut.

DELAWARE

1. Delaware is known as the "First State" because it was the first state to ratify the U.S. Constitution on December 7, 1787.

2. Delaware is the second-smallest state in terms of land area.

3. Rehoboth Beach is known as the "Nation's Summer Capital" due to its popularity as a beach destination.

4. Delaware has the lowest average altitude of any state in the United States.

5. The state's official state flower is the peach blossom.

6. The University of Delaware, established in 1743, is one of the oldest universities in the country.

7. Swedish settlers in Delaware built the first log cabins in North America in 1640.

8. Delaware is one of the few states without any sales tax.

9. Delaware is separated from New Jersey by the Delaware Bay.

10. The Old Swedes Church in Wilmington is one of the oldest churches in the United States, built in 1698.

11. Delaware's other nicknames are the "Diamond State" and "Blue Hen State."

12. Delaware didn't have a National Monument until 2013.

13. The state's official state fish is the weakfish.

14. Lenape Native Americans originally inhabited Delaware.

15. Wilmington, Delaware, is often called the "Chemical Capital of the World" due to its many chemical companies.

16. Pea Patch Island is the site of Fort Delaware, which served as a prisoner-of-war camp during the Civil War.

17. Barratt's Chapel in Kent County, Delaware, is the oldest surviving Methodist church in the United States.

18. Delaware's Old State House in Dover is one of the oldest state capitol buildings still in use.

19. The state is known for its historic covered bridges, such as the Wooddale Covered Bridge.

20. Delaware is often associated with corporate law due to its business-friendly regulations.

21. The city of Lewes was first settled by the Dutch in 1631, making it one of the oldest European settlements in the country.

22. The highest point in Delaware is Ebright Azimuth, reaching just 448 feet (137 meters) above sea level.

23. The Delaware River starts in New York.

24. Delaware did not have a national park until March 25, 2013. First State National Historical Park is located near Wilmington.

25. The Town of Milton, Delaware, was originally called "Head of Broadkiln" when founded in 1763. In 1807, it was renamed Milton in honor of the English Poet John Milton.

26. The DuPont Company, a significant player in the chemical industry, was founded in Delaware in 1802.

27. Delaware was the last state to abolish the use of the whip as a form of punishment in its penal system. It did so in 1972.

28. The Delaware Breakwater at the mouth of the Delaware Bay was the first breakwater in the United States. It was built in 1825 to protect ships from storms.

29. Bob Marley resided in Delaware from 1965 to 1977. Bob also worked for the Dupont Chemical Company during that time.

30. The University of Delaware was home to the country's first study abroad program.

31. The Bombay Hook National Wildlife Refuge is an important stopover for migratory birds along the Atlantic Flyway.

32. The Caesar Rodney Statue in Wilmington commemorates his historic ride to break a tie in the Continental Congress vote for independence.

33. Dover is home to a vibrant Amish community founded in 1915.

34. Delaware Bay is home to the largest population of horseshoe crabs in the world.

35. The state's official state bug is the 7-spotted ladybug.

36. Delaware has only three counties: New Castle, Kent, and Sussex. No state has fewer.

37. Delaware's chicken population outnumbers its human population by almost 200 to 1.

38. Delaware is home to 86 endangered species, including fish, reptiles, amphibians, birds, and mammals.

39. Delaware's internet speeds are the fastest in the country, coming in at an average of 145.8 Mbps. New Jersey and Maryland are a close 2nd and 3rd.

40. Redbird Reef in Delaware is an artificial reef made of subway cars covering 1.3 nautical square miles.

41. Delaware has 11 concrete observation towers along its coast that were built to protect its shores during World War II.

42. Hilary Clinton and Donald Trump own individual companies, listing 1209 North Orange Street as the company's address.

43. From 1638 to 1655, an area of present-day Delaware was known as New Sweden.

44. It took 11 years for European settlers to build a town in what is known today as Delaware.

45. The Bethany Beach firefly can only be found in Delaware.

46. Delaware was named after the first governor of Virginia, Sir Thomas, the twelfth Baron De La Warr.

47. Pea Patch Island was named for an incident in which a ship carrying peas ran aground. The peas that spilled onto the island eventually sprouted and created a pea patch.

48. Delaware is the third most bike-friendly state in the United States.

49. Delaware is home to over one million registered business entities. With a population of just over one million people, that's almost one business per person.

50. Delaware Bay is home to the largest population of horseshoe crabs in the world.

FLORIDA

1. Florida is known as the "Sunshine State" due to its abundant sunshine and warm climate.

2. Florida is 22nd in the United States in terms of land area but 3rd in terms of population.

3. The Florida Everglades is the largest tropical wilderness of any kind in the United States.

4. Walt Disney World Resort, located in Orlando, is the most visited vacation resort in the world.

5. Florida is the only state bordering the Gulf of Mexico and the Atlantic Ocean.

6. The state's official state flower is the orange blossom.

7. Miami is the only major city in the United States that was founded by a woman, Julia Tuttle.

8. Florida is home to the oldest city in the U.S., St. Augustine, founded in 1565 by Spanish Explorers.

9. Key West is the southernmost point in the continental United States.

10. The Florida manatee is the state's official marine mammal.

11. Florida has more golf courses than any other state.

12. The Kennedy Space Center in Cape Canaveral has been the launch site for every U.S. human spaceflight since 1968.

13. The Miami skyline features a distinct architecture known as "MiMo," which stands for Miami Modern.

14. The Florida State Fair in Tampa is one of the oldest state fairs in the U.S.

15. The Florida Panther is one of the most endangered mammals in the world.

16. Florida has the highest number of freshwater springs in the world, many located in state parks.

17. The town of Cassadaga is known as the "Psychic Capital of the World" due to its high concentration of mediums and spiritualists.

18. The state's official state gem is the moonstone.

19. The Ringling Museum of Art in Sarasota, featuring an impressive art collection, was founded by circus magnate John Ringling of Ringling Bros. and Barnum & Bailey Circus fame.

20. The Coral Castle in Homestead is a mysterious structure built by a Latvian immigrant using coral rock.

21. The Florida Keys are known for their stunning coral reefs, making them a popular destination for snorkeling and diving.

22. The Ocala National Forest is the southernmost national forest in the continental U.S.

23. The St. Johns River is one of the few major rivers in the U.S. that flows north.

24. The Florida Keys are connected by a series of bridges and causeways known as the Overseas Highway.

25. Florida has a large retiree population, often called "snowbirds," who migrate south for the winter.

26. The Salvador Dalí Museum in St. Petersburg houses the most extensive collection of Dalí's works outside of Europe.

27. The Miami Art Deco Historic District is known for its pastel-colored architecture from the 1930s.

28. The St. Augustine Alligator Farm Zoological Park is one of the oldest United States zoos, opening in 1893 and focusing on crocodilians.

29. Over two-thirds of Florida's population lives in a coastal area.

30. Florida is the flattest state in the United States, with its highest point being Britton Hill at only 345 feet (105 meters) above sea level.

31. Orlando International Airport is the busiest airport in Florida.

32. The first commercial passenger airline flight was from St. Petersburg to Tampa on January 1, 1914. The flight lasted 23 minutes, and its only passenger was the then-mayor of St. Petersburg, Abraham C. Pheil.

33. Florida is home to the only coral reef barrier in the United States.

34. Florida is home to five types of sea turtles. The Loggerhead, the Green Turtle, the Leatherback, the Hawksbill, and the rarest sea turtle in the world, the Kemp's Ridley.

35. Florida produces more than 70% of all the oranges in America.

36. In 1967, orange juice was chosen as the official state drink.

37. Almost half of the tree species found in the United States can grow in Florida.

38. Florida has the longest shoreline of any contiguous state, measuring 8,436 miles (13,576 kilometers).

39. Florida is home to more than 30,000 lakes.

40. More than 500 native bird species can be found in Florida.

41. Florida leads the United States in thunderstorm activity with 80 to 105+ days a year.

42. South Florida is the only place where you can find alligators and crocodiles living together in the wild.

43. Parallel parking is not tested when getting a driver's license in Florida.

44. Fort Lauderdale is home to a reported 300 miles (265 kilometers) of inland waterways, leading to its nickname "The Venice of America."

45. Florida is home to John Pennekamp Coral Reef State Park, the first undersea park in the United States.

46. In 1963, the city of Carrabelle created the world's smallest police station. The police station is the size of a phone booth and is still on display.

47. The Florida Museum of Natural History houses the world's most extensive collection of butterflies.

48. No point in Florida is more than 60 miles (96.5 kilometers) from the ocean.

49. Key deer, the smallest deer in North America, call Florida home.

50. Six of the ten most visited theme parks are in Florida.

GEORGIA

1. Georgia is known as the "Peach State" due to its historical production of peaches.

2. The state's capital is Atlanta, which is also its largest city.

3. Georgia is home to the world's busiest airport, Hartsfield-Jackson Atlanta International Airport.

4. The state's official state bird is the brown thrasher.

5. Coca-Cola was invented in Atlanta by pharmacist John S. Pemberton in 1886.

6. Georgia is named after King George II of England.

7. The Okefenokee Swamp is one of North America's largest and most well-preserved freshwater ecosystems.

8. Georgia was one of the original 13 colonies and played a crucial role in the American Revolution.

9. The Masters Tournament, one of golf's major championships, is held annually at Augusta National Golf Club.

10. The Georgia Aquarium in Atlanta is the largest aquarium in the world.

11. The University of Georgia was the first state-chartered university in the U.S.

12. The state's official state fruit is the peach.

13. Atlanta hosted the 1996 Summer Olympics.

14. Columbus, Georgia, is home to the National Infantry Museum.

15. Atlanta was admitted to the Union on January 2, 1788. It was the 4th state to join.

16. Georgia is home to Fort Moore (formerly Fort Benning), one of the largest military bases in the U.S.

17. Georgia is the largest state east of the Mississippi River.

18. Outside downtown Atlanta, Stone Mountain is the world's largest solid mass of exposed granite.

19. Georgia shares a border with five other states and the Atlantic Ocean, giving it six borders.

20. Georgia is home to three Native American tribes: the Cherokee of Georgia Tribal, the Georgia Tribe of Eastern Cherokee Reservation, and the Lower Muskogee Creek Tribe.

21. Atlanta, Georgia's state capital, is the state's 5th capital city.

22. Georgia leads the United States in peanut production, with more than 45 percent of all peanuts sold coming from the state.

23. The first gold rush occurred in Georgia, not California.

24. Atlanta's original name was Marthasville, named after the then-governor of Georgia's daughter, Martha.

25. Georgia is home to 383 different species of birds.

26. Wesleyan College in Georgia was the first college in the world to accept women.

27. While states usually have one elected governor, in 1947, Georgia had three for a short period.

28. Georgia was the first state to lower the voting age from 21 to 18.

29. More than 50 percent of the lakes in Georgia are manmade.

30. The original intention for Georgia was for its use as a penal colony.

31. The town of Cordele grows more than 125 million watermelons a year, making it the watermelon capital of the world.

32. Georgia was the first southern state to ratify the constitution.

33. The Varsity, in Atlanta, is the world's largest drive-in fast-food restaurant.

34. The state's official state reptile is the gopher tortoise.

35. Cumberland Island is the largest barrier island off the coast of Georgia and is known for its natural beauty and wild horses.

36. The Georgia Guidestones, often called the "American Stonehenge," are a mysterious granite monument in Elbert County.

37. The Savannah College of Art and Design (SCAD) in Savannah is one of the largest art and design universities in the U.S.

38. The city of Macon hosts the International Cherry Blossom Festival, celebrating its extensive cherry blossom trees.

39. Georgia's Warm Springs was a frequent retreat for President Franklin D. Roosevelt due to its therapeutic springs.

40. The Georgia State Capitol building in Atlanta is covered in gold leaf on its dome, reminiscent of the U.S. Capitol.

41. The town of Helen in the Blue Ridge Mountains is designed to resemble a Bavarian Alpine village.

42. Georgia's 159 counties are more than any other state east of the Mississippi River.

43. Savannah, Georgia, has been ranked as one of the friendliest towns in the United States.

44. Springfield Baptist Church in Augusta is considered the oldest black Baptist congregation in the United States.

Bonus Fact! - It is illegal to place your ice cream in your back pocket on a Sunday.

45. The first Thanksgiving Day observation was in Augusta, Georgia, on July 25, 1742.

46. Some of the most famous scenes from the movie *Forrest Gump* were shot in Savannah, Georgia.

47. Georgia did away with public hangings in 1893.

48. In 1905, Georgia became the first state to recognize a constitutional right to privacy.

49. Berry College in Rome, Georgia, is the world's largest college campus.

50. Eli Whitney invented the cotton gin in Georgia in 1793.

HAWAII

1. Hawaii is the only U.S. state made up entirely of islands.

2. It's located in the Pacific Ocean, about 2,400 miles (3,862 kilometers) southwest of California.

3. Hawaii is the only state with two official languages: English and Hawaiian.

4. The Hawaiian alphabet only has 13 letters, including five vowels and eight consonants.

5. The Big Island of Hawaii is home to Mauna Kea, the tallest mountain on Earth when measured from its base at the ocean floor.

6. The state's official nickname is the "Aloha State."

7. Hawaii is known for its diverse and unique ecosystems, including rainforests, deserts, and coral reefs.

8. The Hawaiian Islands were formed by volcanic activity and continue to grow with active volcanoes.

9. Hawaii is the only U.S. state that grows coffee.

10. Hawaii is one of the best places in the world for stargazing due to its minimal light pollution.

11. The Hawaiian Islands were first settled by Polynesian voyagers around 1,500 years ago.

12. The state's official fish is the humuhumunukunukuapua'a, the reef triggerfish.

13. Hawaii is home to the world's largest dormant volcano, Mount Haleakalā.

14. Hawaii has the highest life expectancy of any state in the U.S.

15. The Hawaiian luau is a traditional feast featuring food, music, hula dancing, and cultural performances.

16. Hawaii is one of the best places for whale-watching, with humpback whales migrating to its warm waters.

17. The island of Molokai is known for having the highest sea cliffs in the world.

18. The USS Arizona Memorial at Pearl Harbor commemorates the events of December 7, 1941.

19. The Hawaiian alphabet does not include B, C, D, Q, R, S, X, or Z.

20. Hawaii has a strong tradition of hula dancing, a cultural practice that tells stories through movement and music.

21. The Hawaiian Islands are home to many endemic species found nowhere else on Earth.

22. The state's official gem is the black coral.

23. The Mauna Kea Observatories on the Big Island are some of the world's most important astronomical research centers.

24. Mauna Loa is considered the largest subaerial volcano in the world. The only volcano larger is Tamu Massif; however, Tamu Massif's summit is 6,500 feet (1,981 meters) below the ocean's surface.

25. The state's official tree is the kukui tree, also known as the candlenut tree.

26. The islands were united into a single kingdom by King Kamehameha I in the early 19th century.

27. Hawaii has the highest percentage of Asian Americans and Pacific Islanders in the U.S.

28. The Iolani Palace in Honolulu is the only royal palace in the United States.

29. Hawaii was the 50th state to join the Union, achieving statehood on August 21, 1959.

30. The Aloha Spirit Law encourages Hawaiians to promote the principles of aloha, unity, and love.

31. Hawaii is made up of 137 islands. However, most people refer to the eight largest when referring to Hawaii: Hawaii (the Big Island, Maui, Oahu, Kauai, Molokai, Lanai, Niihau, and Kahoolawe.

32. Hawaii does not observe daylight savings time.

33. A 27-foot-tall obelisk on the Big Island marks where the English Captain James Cook was killed; the United Kingdom technically owns the land that the obelisk sits on.

34. Lahainaluna High School on Maui is the oldest school west of the Rocky Mountains, established in 1831.

35. The sport of surfing was invented by ancient Hawaiians hundreds of years ago.

36. NASA uses the lava fields of Mauna Loa to train its astronauts.

37. The first nonstop flight from Hawaii to the Mainland landed in June 1927, having taken off 26 hours prior from Oakland. The name of the plane was the *Bird of Paradise*.

38. In 1959, 94.3 percent of Hawaii's population voted to join the United States as a state.

39. Hawaii is the only state that doesn't lie on the continent of North America. Its location technically puts it in Oceania.

40. The post office in Hawaii will allow you to send a coconut as a postcard.

41. Ka Lae, located on the Big Island, is the most southern point in America.

42. The world's largest pineapple maze is on the Dole Pineapple Plantation in Oahu.

43. Hawaii does not allow billboards as it takes away from the views.

44. Less than 15 percent of the world's pineapples come from Hawaii.

45. On the island of Kauai, it is illegal to build a building taller than a palm tree; for this reason, no building can be more than four stories tall.

46. It rains on Mount Waialeale on Kauai every day, amounting to nearly 400 inches of rain annually.

47. Hawaii has no native species of snakes.

48. Hawaii's official state mammal is the Hawaiian monk seal.

49. The annual Merrie Monarch Festival in Hilo celebrates traditional Hawaiian hula and culture.

50. Hawaii is the second widest state in the U.S. at 1,523 miles (2,451 kilometers) between east and west. Alaska is almost twice as wide, reaching 2,700 miles (4,345 kilometers).

IDAHO

1. Idaho is known as the "Gem State" due to its abundant natural resources and gemstones.

2. Idaho was originally part of Oregon and Washington. It became the Territory of Idaho in 1863, and in 1890, it was the 43rd state admitted to the Union.

3. Idaho is home to the deepest river gorge in North America, Hells Canyon, which is deeper than the Grand Canyon.

4. Idaho's state bird is the mountain bluebird.

5. America's first ski resort, Sun Valley Resort, opened in Ketchum, Idaho, in 1936.

6. The state's official state fish is the cutthroat trout.

7. The Idaho State Capitol building is the only one in the United States that is heated by geothermal energy.

8. Craters of the Moon National Monument and Preserve features a volcanic landscape resembling the moon's surface.

9. Shoshone Falls, located near Twin Falls, is higher than Niagara Falls and is often called the "Niagara of the West."

10. The world's first nuclear power plant to produce electricity for a power grid was built in Idaho in 1951. The plant was in Atomic City, Idaho, and named Experimental Breeder Reactor I (EBR-I), and was decommissioned in 1964.

11. Idaho has a significant Basque population, particularly in Boise, with a vibrant Basque culture. It is the largest Basqu population outside of Spain and France.

12. The Craters of the Moon lava fields served as a training ground for Apollo astronauts preparing for moon missions.

13. The state's official state insect is the monarch butterfly.

14. Idaho is home to the iconic Sun Valley Film Festival, attracting filmmakers and enthusiasts from around the world.

15. The state's official state vegetable is the potato.

16. The Teton Dam, which failed in 1976, resulted in catastrophic flooding but led to improvements in dam safety regulations.

17. The town of Wallace is famous for having the Center of the Universe, marked by a manhole cover.

18. Idaho comes from a Native American term meaning "the gem of the Mountains."

19. Idaho is home to over 240 different types of precious stones and minerals.

20. Nearly one-third of America's potatoes come from Idaho.

21. Idaho is home to the largest potato in the world. The potato functions as an Airbnb.

22. Despite its potato notoriety, Idaho is known as the Lentil Capital of the World.

23. Idaho spans two time zones: the Mountain Time Zone and the Pacific Time Zone.

24. Roosevelt Grove of Ancient Cedars features trees that are 2,000 years old.

25. Most of the energy consumed in Idaho is imported from other states.

26. If you measured all the rivers in Idaho, it would be longer than 105,000 miles (168.981 kilometers).

27. The state seal of Idaho was designed by a woman, the only state seal to hold this distinction.

28. It is illegal to not smile in Pocatello, Idaho.

29. Idaho is home to Heaven's Gate lookout, a spot where you can see Washington, Montana, and Oregon from a single location.

30. The St. Joe River is the highest navigable river in the world at an elevation of almost 7,000 feet (2,133 meters).

31. Idaho has more whitewater river miles than any other state.

32. Idaho is home to the Silver Mountain Resort in Kellogg, which proudly offers the longest gondola ride in the United States. The gondola travels 3.1 miles (4,989 meters).

33. The Lake Coeur d'Alene boardwalk is the longest floating boardwalk in the world, coming in at 3,300 feet (1,005 meters).

34. The city of Island Park has the longest main street in the United States.

35. Public land accounts for 63 percent of the land in Idaho.

36. Around 70 percent of commercial trout sold in the United States comes from Hagerman Valley.

37. In 1928, the word "potato" appeared on the state's license plate.

38. Idaho is home to the port of Lewiston, 465 miles (748 kilometers) from the ocean; it is the most inland seaport on the West Coast.

39. Idaho is home to several natural hot springs, including those in Lava Hot Springs.

40. The Lewis and Clark Expedition traveled through parts of present-day Idaho on their westward journey.

41. The Salmon River, also known as the "River of No Return," is one of the longest free-flowing rivers in the U.S.

42. Idaho is the third largest cheese producer in the United States.

43. The town of Twin Falls is named after a nearby waterfall on the Snake River.

44. Idaho is home to a large population of eagles, and the annual Eagle Watch Festival celebrates these majestic birds.

45. The Idaho Potato Drop is a New Year's Eve event in Boise where a giant potato descends instead of a ball.

46. The state is home to the National Oldtime Fiddlers' Contest and Festival in Weiser.

47. More than half of the population of Idaho lives in the Boise metro area.

48. Idaho has the largest wilderness area in the lower 48 states, the Frank Church—River of No Return Wilderness.

49. Bonners Ferry, Idaho, is home to the world's largest contiguous hops farm. Elk Mountain Farm is over 1,700 acres (688 hectares).

50. On August 13, 1896, renowned bandits Butch Cassidy and the Wild Bunch Gang held up a bank in Montpelier, Idaho, reportedly managing to escape with $7,165 (the equivalent of $249,940 thousand in 2023). This bank remains the sole surviving establishment from the series of bank heists across the country.

ILLINOIS

1. Illinois is known as the "Land of Lincoln" because it's the state where Abraham Lincoln lived for most of his life.

2. Chicago, the state's largest city, is famous for its deep-dish pizza and vibrant arts scene.

3. The world's first skyscraper, the Home Insurance Building, was constructed in Chicago in 1885. The building was originally ten stories high, with two more floors being added in 1891. Its finished height was 180 feet (54.9 kilometers) tall.

4. The official state bird of Illinois is the northern cardinal.

5. The Sears Tower in Chicago (now known as the Willis Tower) was the tallest building in the world for many years. The Willis Tower stands at 1,451 feet (442 meters) tall and has 110 floors.

6. The Chicago River was famously dyed green for the city's St. Patrick's Day celebrations.

7. The University of Chicago was the site of the first controlled nuclear chain reaction in 1942.

8. The state's official state animal is the white-tailed deer.

9. The Illinois State Fair is one of the longest-running state fairs in the United States.

10. The Art Institute of Chicago is one of the oldest and largest art museums in the United States. The museum was founded in 1879.

11. The state's official state fossil is the Tully monster, a prehistoric marine creature.

12. Illinois is home to a stretch of the famous Route 66, the "Main Street of America."

13. The Chicago "L" is the second-busiest rapid transit system in the United States and the fourth-largest in terms of total route length. Only the New York City Subway is busier.

14. The state's official state fish is the bluegill.

15. The Illinois River is a major tributary of the Mississippi River.

16. The Field Museum in Chicago is known for its extensive collection of natural history exhibits and is one of the largest natural history museums in the world.

17. The Chicago Public Library has 81 branches.

18. The Adler Planetarium in Chicago was the first planetarium in the Western Hemisphere.

19. Illinois was the first state to ratify the 13th Amendment, abolishing slavery.

20. The Chicago Water Tower is one of the few structures to survive the Great Chicago Fire of 1871.

21. The Pullman Historic District in Chicago is a preserved model industrial town.

22. The Illinois State Capitol in Springfield features an impressive Renaissance-style dome.

23. The Chicago Cultural Center is the first free municipal cultural center in the United States.

24. The Illinois State Police, formed on April 1, 1922, is one of the country's oldest state law enforcement agencies.

25. Chicago is the 3rd largest city in the United States.

26. The iconic city of Chicago is known as the "Windy City."

27. The Illinois State Flower, the violet, was chosen in 1908 as a symbol of loyalty and faithfulness.

28. Illinois is the birthplace of the fast-food chain McDonald's, which started in Des Plaines.

29. The Field Museum in Chicago is home to "Sue," the largest and most complete Tyrannosaurus rex fossil ever discovered.

30. The Mississippi River flows more through Illinois than any other state.

31. The Chicago River flows backward due to a historic engineering project that reversed its course to prevent pollution from Lake Michigan.

32. George Ferris built the world's first Ferris wheel for the 1893 World's Columbian Exposition in Chicago.

33. The Chicago Cultural Center boasts the world's largest Tiffany glass dome, spanning 38 feet in diameter.

34. Illinois is home to the Chicago Botanic Garden, which features over 385 acres of themed gardens and plant collections.

35. Illinois is known for its robust agricultural industry, producing over 90% of the nation's pumpkin crop.

36. Starved Rock State Park in Oglesby features stunning canyons, waterfalls, and scenic overlooks along the Illinois River.

37. The Chicago Air and Water Show is one of the largest free airshows in the United States, attracting thousands of spectators.

38. The Lincoln Park Zoo in Chicago is the fourth oldest zoo in the United States, founded in 1868.

39. Galena, Illinois, around 160 miles (257.5 kilometers) northwest of Chicago, was once the largest city in Illinois, with a population of around 10,000 in the late 1820s.

40. No Civil War battles were fought in Illinois despite being a Union state.

41. The Nabisco factory in Chicago is the world's largest bakery, occupying around 1.8 million square feet (167,225 square meters).

42. Illinois is home to the Chicago Symphony Orchestra, one of the most acclaimed orchestras in the world.

43. The Bahá'í House of Worship, situated in Wilmette, Illinois, serves as the primary temple for the Bahá'í Faith in North America. Having been constructed in 1912, it was the second Bahá'í temple ever created, following one in Turkmenistan that no longer exists.

Consequently, the Illinois temple holds the distinction of being the world's oldest existing Bahá'í temple.

44. The Cahokia Mounds State Historic Site contains the largest pre-Columbian settlement north of Mexico.

45. Illinois ranks second among the top corn-producing states in the U.S., contributing to various products like ethanol and animal feed. The only state that produces more is Iowa.

46. The state's official snack, popcorn, is celebrated during the annual Popcorn Festival in Marion.

47. Between 1923 and 1969, the designated state language of Illinois wasn't English but rather "American."

48. John Deere founded Deere & Company in 1837 in Grand Detour, Illinois.

49. Softball's origins can be traced back to Chicago, Illinois, where it emerged as a derivative of indoor baseball.

50. Around three-fourths of Illinois is farmland.

INDIANA

1. Indiana is often called the "Hoosier State," and the origin of the term "Hoosier" remains a topic of debate.

2. Indiana is known for its beautiful, covered bridges, with the Parke County area being particularly famous for having the highest number of covered bridges in the state.

3. The name Indiana means "Land of the Indians."

4. The Indianapolis 500, one of the world's most famous and prestigious car races, occurs annually at the Indianapolis Motor Speedway.

5. Indiana was the 19th state admitted to the union on December 11, 1816.

6. Santa Claus, Indiana, is known for its festive holiday spirit and receives thousands of letters addressed to Santa Claus each year.

7. West Baden Springs, Indiana, is home to the historic West Baden Springs Hotel, known for its elaborate dome and architecture.

8. The iconic Coca-Cola bottle design, known as the "contour bottle," was created by the Root Glass Company of Terre Haute, Indiana.

9. In 2016, wild bison were brought to Indiana in an attempt to repopulate the state. There are currently over 90 bison in Indiana.

10. The Indianapolis Zoo is one of the first zoos in the nation to receive international accreditation.

11. Wabash, Indiana, is home to the first electrically lit city in the world, an accomplishment achieved in 1880.

12. The "World's Largest Sycamore Stump" can be found in Kokomo, Indiana, serving as a quirky roadside attraction. The stump is 57 feet (17 meters) in diameter.

13. The town of Marengo features Marengo Cave, a natural limestone cave system that attracts visitors with its stunning formations.

14. Indiana's state insect is the Say's firefly, recognized for its bioluminescent glow.

15. The USS LST 325, a World War II landing ship, is permanently docked in Evansville as a museum and memorial.

16. The Soldiers' and Sailors' Monument in downtown Indianapolis is the largest outdoor memorial of its kind in the United States.

17. The Indianapolis Motor Speedway has more than 250,000 permanent seats, making it the highest-capacity sports venue in the world.

18. The oldest continually inhabited European settlement in Indiana is Vincennes, having been established in 1732 by French fur traders.

19. The Indianapolis Museum of Art at Newfields is one of the oldest and largest general art museums in the United States. The museum opened in 1883.

20. The Garfield Trail in Grant County features 14 larger-than-life statues of the fictional cat character Garfield.

21. Indiana's state song, "On the Banks of the Wabash, Far Away," is one of the oldest state songs in the United States. The piece was published in 1897.

22. The city of South Bend is known for the University of Notre Dame and its iconic Golden Dome.

23. The town of Jasper is known for its annual Strassenfest, celebrating German heritage and culture.

24. Indiana's state ship was the USS Indiana (BB-1), a battleship commissioned in 1895.

25. Elvis Presley's last concert was at Market Square Arena in Indianapolis three months before he died in 1977.

26. Indiana is the leading producer of popcorn in the United States.

27. The first-ever train robbery occurred in Jackson County, Indiana, on October 6, 1866.

28. Louis J. Koch opened Santa Claus Land in 1946 in Santa Claus, Indiana. Today, the park is known as Holiday World & Splashin' Safari.

29. Over 200,000 Union soldiers came from Indiana during the Civil War.

30. The first gasoline pump was invented in Fort Wayne, Indiana, by Sylvanus Bowser on September 5, 1885.

31. The Children's Museum of Indianapolis is the largest children's museum in the world.

32. The Wabash River is the longest free-flowing river east of the Mississippi River.

33. The world's largest ball of paint, created by layering paint on a baseball, can be found in Alexandria, Indiana.

34. Indiana's state flag has 13 stars to represent the original 13 colonies.

35. The town of Story, Indiana, is often considered one of the smallest towns in the country, with a population of around 2.

36. The world's most extensive collection of Kurt Vonnegut memorabilia can be found at the Kurt Vonnegut Museum and Library in Indianapolis.

37. The "Little 500" bicycle race at Indiana University is one of the largest and most competitive collegiate bike races.

38. The Indiana Statehouse in Indianapolis is topped with a bronze statue of the state's namesake, the goddess Indiana.

39. The West Baden Springs Hotel features a spectacular dome known as the "Eighth Wonder of the World" and was once the largest free-standing dome in the world.

40. Indiana has sand dunes and a national park dedicated to them. The Indiana Dunes National Park is 20 miles (32 kilometers) long along Lake Michigan.

41. The Indianapolis Zoo is the first zoo in the United States to be triple accredited as a zoo, aquarium, and botanical garden.

42. The Rotary Jail in Crawfordsville is a unique, rotary-style jail that allowed guards to rotate cells to the building's exterior for inmate access.

43. The Studebaker, an iconic car, was founded in Indiana in 1852. The Studebaker National Museum is in South Bend, Indiana.

44. Parts of Indiana have switched back and forth between Eastern and Central time zones.

45. Corydon, Indiana, was the state's first capital, and its historic district includes the original state capitol building.

46. It is illegal to force a monkey to smoke a cigarette in South Bend, Indiana.

47. Indiana's state stone is Indiana limestone, widely used in architecture and monuments across the state.

48. Indiana's state seal was first adopted in 1816, but it didn't become official until 1963.

49. Indiana is among the few states without an official state mammal or state fish.

50. From 1900 to 1920, Indiana was responsible for producing more than 170 different makes of cars.

IOWA

1. Iowa is known as the "Hawkeye State," after the fictional character Hawkeye from James Fenimore Cooper's novel *The Last of the Mohicans*.

2. The world's largest strawberry, built to honor the state's strawberry crop, can be found in Strawberry Point, Iowa. The statue stands 15 feet (4.6 meters) tall.

3. A small house in Eldon, Iowa, inspired the iconic American Gothic painting by Grant Wood.

4. Iowa became the 29th state to join the Union on December 28, 1846.

5. The Butter Cow, a famous butter sculpture, is a traditional attraction at the Iowa State Fair.

6. The Iowa State Capitol in Des Moines is one of only a few state capitol buildings with five domes.

7. The world's largest truck stop, Iowa 80, is in Walcott and sits on 220 acres (89 hectares).

8. The state bird of Iowa is the eastern goldfinch.

9. The Amana Colonies, established by German immigrants, are known for their unique communal living history.

10. The first electronic computer, the Atanasoff-Berry Computer, was developed at Iowa State University by John Vincent Atanasoff.

11. Iowa's Loess Hills are unique geological formations created by wind-blown soil deposits.

12. The Bridges of Madison County, famous from the novel and film of the same name, are located in Iowa.

13. The Iowa State Fair's famous "Food-on-a-Stick" tradition features various creative foods skewered for easy consumption.

14. The National Czech & Slovak Museum & Library in Cedar Rapids showcases Czech and Slovak heritage.

15. The *Field of Dreams* movie site in Dyersville attracts baseball fans from around the world.

16. The town of Eldora is home to the Hardin County Historic Courthouse, the oldest courthouse in continuous use in Iowa. The courthouse was built in 1892.

17. The first caucuses of the presidential election season are held in Iowa.

18. The Surf Ballroom in Clear Lake is famous as the last place Buddy Holly, Ritchie Valens, and J.P. Richardson performed before their fatal plane crash.

19. The Effigy Mounds National Monument contains more than 200 prehistoric mounds shaped like animals and other forms.

20. The RAGBRAI (Register's Annual Great Bicycle Ride Across Iowa) is the world's oldest, largest, and longest recreational bicycle touring event. The first RAGBRAI was held in 1973.

21. The Grotto of the Redemption in West Bend is a series of nine grottos depicting scenes from the life of Jesus.

22. Iowa's state flower is the prairie rose.

23. The Iowa State University campus boasts the beautiful Campanile, a 50-bell carillon.

24. The first public college of veterinary medicine was established by Iowa State University in 1879.

25. Iowa produces more eggs than any other state, with around 17 billion eggs per year.

26. The town of Elk Horn has the only working Danish windmill in the U.S.

27. More than 30 million acres of land in Iowa is dedicated to farming.

28. Peru, Iowa, is the birthplace of the Red Delicious apple.

29. In 1930, George Nissen invented the trampoline in Blairstown, Iowa.

30. The Effigy Mounds National Monument's mounds are believed to have been constructed between A.D. 750 and 1250.

31. The Iowa State Capitol's dome is covered in 23-karat gold leaf.

32. The University of Iowa is recognized as the place where the butterfly stroke originated. The butterfly stroke technique was developed by head swim coach Dave Armbruster in 1935.

33. There are nine different species of bats in Iowa.

34. Over half of Iowa's electricity comes from wind generation.

35. Iowa is bordered by six other states: Nebraska, Illinois, Wisconsin, Missouri, South Dakota, and Minnesota.

36. Snake Alley in Burlington, Iowa, is one of the most crooked streets in the world.

37. Sloths used to call Iowa home. Unfortunately, they became extinct around 9,500 years ago.

38. Jim Glasgow created a 16-foot wooden nickel that sits off Iowa Interstate 80 as a form of protest.

39. Bonnie and Clyde, the infamous duo, once found themselves in a shootout in Dexter, Iowa.

40. In Iowa, you'll find the biggest non-governmental seed bank in the United States.

41. The first female lawyer in the United States, Arabella Mansfield, was admitted to practice law in Iowa.

42. Iowa is home to the world's largest Bullhead Statute at 12 feet long (3.66 meters).

43. There are more pigs in Iowa than there are humans. Iowa is home to more than 23 million hogs and pigs.

44. Iowa was the birthplace of the initial bread-slicing machine created by Otto Frederick Rohwedder.

45. Iowa is uniquely the sole state bordered by two rivers suitable for navigation: the Missouri River to the west and the Mississippi River to the east. These rivers fully define the state's eastern and western boundaries.

46. Iowa is the only state name that begins with two consecutive vowels.

47. Iowa is home to Elwood, the world's tallest Gnome, standing 15 feet (4.57) tall and weighing over 3,500 pounds (1,587.6 kilograms).

48. More than 82 percent of Iowa's population is Christian.

49. In Dubuque, the Fenelon Place Elevator is situated along 4th Street and is known as the shortest and steepest scenic railway. Ascending 296 feet, it transports passengers from Fourth Street to Fenelon Place across a distance of 189 feet. This attraction provides breathtaking panoramic vistas of the Mississippi River and spans three states.

50. The largest concrete bull, Albert, can be found in Iowa. Standing at the height of 28 feet (8.5 meters) and boasting a 15-foot (4.57 meters) gap between its horns, this monumental bull was erected in Audubon in 1964 and weighs a substantial 45 tons (40,823 kilograms).

KANSAS

1. Kansas is known as the "Sunflower State" due to its abundant wild sunflowers.

2. The state's motto is "Ad astra per aspera," meaning "To the stars through difficulties."

3. Kansas was named after the Kansa Native American tribe that inhabited the region.

4. The first permanent white settlement in Kansas was established in 1827 at Fort Leavenworth.

5. Dodge City was a famous Wild West town known for its lawlessness and cowboy culture.

6. Kansas was a battleground during the Civil War due to its divided views on slavery.

7. The town of Liberal is home to the International Pancake Day Race, where participants run while flipping pancakes.

8. The state has more than 10,000 miles (16,093 kilometers) of streams and rivers.

9. The world's largest ball of twine is in Cawker City, Kansas.

10. The iconic *The Wizard of Oz* movie was set in Kansas, as depicted in the opening scenes.

11. The state's official animal is the American buffalo.

12. The Kansas State Capitol in Topeka is topped with a dome covered in 22-karat gold leaf.

13. Kansas has the largest population of wild grouse in North America.

14. The city of Wichita is known as the "Air Capital of the World" due to its aviation industry.

15. The Underground Salt Museum in Hutchinson offers tours of an underground salt mine.

16. Greensburg's Big Well is the world's largest hand-dug well, measuring 109 feet deep and 32 feet in diameter.

17. Kansas was a major stop on the Santa Fe Trail, an important trade route in the 19th century.

18. Kansas is one of the top wheat-producing states in the U.S., with over seven million acres (28,327 square kilometers) devoted to growing the crop.

19. Lucas's *Garden of Eden* is an unusual folk art environment created by S.P. Dinsmoor.

20. The world's most extensive memorabilia collection from the Wizard of Oz can be found in Wamego, Kansas.

21. Nicodemus, founded in 1877, is the only remaining western town established by African Americans during Reconstruction.

22. Kansas has many prairie ecosystems, with tallgrass, mixed-grass, and shortgrass prairies.

23. The state's official fish is the channel catfish, found in many of Kansas' waterways.

24. The "Dorothy's House and Land of Oz" attraction in Liberal recreates scenes from *The Wizard of Oz*.

25. Amelia Earhart's childhood home in Atchison is now a museum dedicated to her legacy.

26 The Museum of World Treasures in Wichita features a diverse collection of artifacts from around the world.

27. The Brown v. Board of Education National Historic Site in Topeka commemorates the landmark Supreme Court case that ended school segregation.

28. Kansas ranks as one of the top wind energy-producing states in the U.S.

29. The Sunflower State is home to the Konza Prairie Biological Station in Manhattan, Kansas, a preserve for native tallgrass prairie.

30. The Gypsum Hills in south-central Kansas are known for their distinctive red and orange rock formations.

31. Monument Rocks in western Kansas is a unique geological formation often called the "Chalk Pyramids."

32. The Tallgrass Prairie National Preserve in the Flint Hills is one of the last remaining areas of tallgrass prairie in the U.S.

33. The rock band Kansas is from Topeka, Kansas.

34. Kansas has a rich agricultural heritage, and is known as the "Breadbasket of the Nation."

35. The Hollenberg Pony Express Station in Hanover is a historic site that was a crucial stop on the Pony Express route.

36. The Sedgwick County Zoo in Wichita is one of the largest zoos in the U.S.

37. Several cities in Kansas average higher wind speeds than Chicago, which is traditionally known as the "Windy City."

38. Around 10 percent of all meteorites in the United States are found in Kansas.

39. Kansas holds claim to the largest grain elevator in the world. The grain elevator in Wichita, Kansas, is 2,657 feet (809.8 meters) long and can hold 22.4 million bushels of grain.

40. Icee, the popular summertime treat, was created in Coffeyville, Kansas.

41. The highest point in Kansas is Mount Sunflower, 4,039 feet (1,231 meters) above sea level.

42. The Blue Sky Sculpture in Wichita is a unique public art installation that depicts a picturesque blue sky with clouds.

43. The city of Topeka's name comes from a Kansa-Osage word meaning "place where we dig potatoes."

44. The first Pizza Hut was built in 1958 in Wichita, Kansas.

45. The town of Lucas features the World's Largest Collection of the World's Smallest Versions of the World's Largest Things.

46. The C.W. Parker Carousel Museum in Leavenworth showcases historic carousels and amusement rides.

47. The OZtoberFest in Wamego is an annual *The Wizard of Oz*-themed event.

48. The geographic center of the contiguous United States is located near Lebanon, Kansas.

49. The Orphan Train Museum in Concordia tells the story of orphaned children placed in new homes across the U.S.

50. More than 88% of Kansas' total land area is dedicated to farmland, with only Texas and Montana having larger proportions of agricultural land.

KENTUCKY

1. Kentucky is known as the "Bluegrass State" due to the abundance of bluegrass that grows there.

2. The state's capital, Frankfort, is the fourth-smallest state capital in the U.S. by population.

3. Kentucky is famous for its bourbon production and is home to the Bourbon Trail.

4. The Kentucky Derby, held annually at Churchill Downs in Louisville, is one of the most famous horse races in the world and the first leg of the Triple Crown.

5. Mammoth Cave National Park is home to the world's longest-known cave system.

6. Kentucky is known for its picturesque rolling hills and horse farms.

7. The Corvette is a famous American sports car manufactured in Bowling Green, Kentucky.

8. Abraham Lincoln was born in a log cabin in Hardin County, now part of Kentucky.

9. The Louisville Slugger baseball bat is produced in Louisville.

10. Kentucky is home to several important Civil War battlefields, including Perryville and Mill Springs.

11. The world's largest baseball bat is at the Louisville Slugger Museum in Louisville, Kentucky. The bat is 120 feet (36.6 meters) tall and made to resemble the bat used by Babe Ruth.

12. Colonel Harland Sanders was born in Henryville, Indiana, but developed his famous KFC fried chicken recipe in Kentucky.

13. Kentucky is home to over 90 distilleries that produce bourbon.

14. Bluegrass music, characterized by its unique picking style, has its roots in Kentucky.

15. The Louisville Mega Cavern is a former limestone mine turned into an underground adventure park.

16. The birthplace of Muhammad Ali, "The Greatest," is Louisville.

17. The International Bluegrass Music Museum is in Owensboro.

18. The state's official dance is the clogging dance.

19. Kentucky has a diverse geography, including mountains, rolling hills, and flat plains.

20. The Muhammad Ali Center in Louisville honors the boxer's life and achievements.

21. The state's official musical instrument is the Appalachian dulcimer.

22. Kentucky is home to the Belle of Louisville, one of the oldest operating steamboats in the U.S.

23. The National Corvette Museum in Bowling Green showcases the iconic car's history.

24. The Harland Sanders Café and Museum in Corbin is a KFC museum located at the site of the original restaurant.

25. The Kentucky Bourbon Festival is an annual event celebrating the state's bourbon heritage.

26. The Waverly Hills Sanatorium in Louisville is known for its haunted history.

27. The state's official horse is the thoroughbred, renowned for racing and equestrian sports.

28. The Ark Encounter in Williamstown features a life-sized replica of Noah's Ark.

29. The National Quilt Museum in Paducah showcases intricate and artistic quilt designs.

30. The National Horse Show, one of the oldest horse shows in the U.S., is held in Kentucky.

31. Kentucky was once part of Virginia before becoming its own state.

32. The Kentucky State Capitol in Frankfort features a dome inspired by the United States Capitol.

33. Fort Knox was named after Henry Knox, a Revolutionary War general and the first United States Secretary of War. The military camp at Fort Knox was established in 1918 during World War I.

34. The Kentucky Derby is the world's oldest continuously held horse race. The first race was held on May 17, 1875.

35. The lightbulb was introduced to the world by Thomas Edison at the 1883 Southern Exposition held in Louisville.

36. Up until 1997, when 3M's patent on the Post-it note expired, Post-it notes were only created in Cynthiana, Kentucky.

37. The world's largest collection of ventriloquist dummies can be found at the Vent Haven Museum in Fort Mitchell.

38. At the Kentucky Vietnam Veterans Memorial located in Frankfort, the shadow of a massive sundial contacts the name of every veteran on the specific day they passed away.

39. Georgetown, Kentucky, is home to the world's biggest Toyota manufacturing facility. This factory holds the distinction of being the first entirely U.S.-owned Toyota vehicle plant and serves as the production site for the Camry, Lexus ES 350, and Avalon models. The manufacturing plant can produce 550,000 vehicles a year.

40. Fort Knox, located in Kentucky, is famous for housing a significant portion of the United States' gold reserves.

41. The Cumberland Falls in Corbin is known as the "Niagara of the South."

42. Middlesboro, Kentucky, is built inside a crater.

43. The origins of Mother's Day can be linked to Henderson. During the 1880s, a teacher named Mary Towles Sasseen Wilson was acknowledged for commemorating her mother on that occasion. From 1916 onward, it has been established as an official holiday.

44. The Jif peanut butter production plant in Lexington, Kentucky, is the world's largest peanut butter production plant.

45. A distinct portion of Kentucky is not physically connected to the rest of the state. Approximately 17 square miles are situated along the Mississippi River, linked to Tennessee. This unique geographical anomaly, called the Kentucky Bend, resulted from a surveying mistake. Only 17 individuals reside in this area, and reaching the remainder of the state requires a 40-mile journey.

46. While it's often associated with gold storage, Fort Knox is primarily a military installation. It serves as a training center for various Army units and is home to the United States Army Armor School and the Army Human Resources Command.

47. Newport, Kentucky, is home to the World Peace Bell, one of more than 20 Peace Bells worldwide and one of the largest free-swinging bells in the world.

48. Cumberland Falls is the only location in the Western Hemisphere where one can witness a moonbow. This distinctive lunar rainbow emerges when moonlight interacts with water droplets during nighttime.

49. Richmond, Kentucky, was named after Richmond, Virginia.

50. Pikeville, Kentucky, leads the nation in per capita consumption of Pepsi.

The Big Book of State Facts

LOUISIANA

1. Louisiana is known as the "Pelican State" due to the brown pelican's presence along its coast.

2. Louisiana is the only state in the United States with political subdivisions called "parishes" instead of counties.

3. New Orleans is famous for its Mardi Gras celebrations, the largest and most well-known in the United States.

4. The city of New Orleans was founded by the French in 1718.

5. Jazz, a unique American musical genre, originated in New Orleans.

6. Louisiana is home to the longest continuous bridge over water in the world: the Lake Pontchartrain Causeway.

7. The French Quarter in New Orleans is one of the oldest neighborhoods in the country.

8. Louisiana is the only state in the United States that practices civil law, which has been derived from the French Napoleonic Code. The rest of the United States practice common law derived from British common law.

9. The Louisiana Purchase doubled the size of the United States when it was acquired from France in 1803.

10. The state has diverse cultures, including French, Spanish, African, and Native American influences.

11. Louisiana is known for its Creole and Cajun cuisines, famous for dishes like gumbo, jambalaya, and crawfish étouffée.

12. Tabasco sauce is a popular hot sauce produced on Avery Island in Louisiana.

13. The Louisiana Superdome, now known as the Caesars Superdome, was the largest enclosed stadium in the world when it opened in 1975.

14. Louisiana was the 18th state admitted to the Union. It joined on April 30, 1812.

15. The state's official dog is the Catahoula Leopard Dog.

16. The historic St. Charles Avenue streetcar line in New Orleans is one of the world's oldest continuously operating streetcar lines.

17. The city of Natchitoches, founded in 1714, is the oldest permanent settlement in the Louisiana Purchase territory.

18. Baton Rouge, the capital, translates from French as "Red Stick," supposedly referring to a red cypress tree used as a boundary marker by Native Americans.

19. There are more alligators in Louisiana than in any other state. The state is home to more than two million alligators.

20. Louisiana is home to unique wildlife, including alligators, nutria, and various bird species.

21. The town of Rayne is known as the "Frog Capital of the World."

22. The annual French Quarter Festival is one of the largest free music festivals in the United States.

23. The city of Lafayette is known as the "Hub City" due to its location at the crossroads of major highways.

24. Louisiana has a rich history of voodoo practices and traditions, particularly in New Orleans.

25. Lake Pontchartrain, a large estuary, is connected to the Gulf of Mexico through the Rigolets and Chef Menteur Pass.

26. The Louisiana State Capitol in Baton Rouge is the tallest capitol building in the United States. The building is 450 feet (137 meters) high and has 34 floors.

27. The Chitimacha Tribe of Louisiana is recognized as one of the oldest Native American tribes in the state.

28. Louisiana has its own distinct style of country music known as "Swamp Pop."

29. The town of Breaux Bridge is known as the "Crawfish Capital of the World."

30. Poverty Point State Historic Site features one of North America's most significant prehistoric archaeological sites.

31. The Louisiana Old State Capitol, known for its distinctive Neo-Gothic medieval-style castle architecture, now serves as a museum.

32. Jazz funerals in New Orleans are unique cultural events that blend mourning with musical celebration.

33. The Battle of New Orleans, fought on January 8, 1815, was after the War of 1812 had officially ended and became a major American victory over the British Army.

34. The Tchefuncte River is one of the shortest rivers in the world, flowing only about 70 miles.

35. The Acadian people, known as Cajuns, were exiled from Canada and became an integral part of Louisiana's culture.

36. The Toledo Bend Reservoir on the Louisiana-Texas border is one of the largest man-made reservoirs in the United States.

37. The Baton Rouge Zoo has over 1,800 animals and various interactive exhibits.

38. The city of Lake Charles is known for its annual Contraband Days festival, celebrating its pirate history.

39. The state's official beverage is milk.

40. The city of Ruston is home to the annual Louisiana Peach Festival.

41. Louisiana was home to the first indoor movie theater in the world, Vitascope Hall, in 1896.

42. The mixed cocktail was born in Louisiana. The Sazerac was created by Antoine Amédée Peychaud in New Orleans in 1838.

43. Due to the city of New Orleans being built below sea level, cemeteries in the city are above ground.

44. Louisiana was named in honor of the French King Louis XIV.

45. New Orleans is known to be the "Most Haunted City in America."

46. Louisiana was purchased from France in 1803 for $15 million, the equivalent of $405 million in 2023.

47. The Whitney Plantation in Edgard, Louisiana, is one of the only plantations whose mission is to educate the public about slavery in the Southern United States.

48. The Louisiana State Penitentiary, known as Angola Prison, is the largest maximum-security prison in the United States.

49. Louisiana is home to one of the oldest active Jewish congregations in the United States, Temple Sinai in New Orleans. The temple was founded in 1870.

50. The Natchitoches Christmas Festival is one of Louisiana's oldest and most celebrated holiday events.

MAINE

1. Maine is known as the "Pine Tree State" due to its extensive forests.

2. It's the easternmost state in the contiguous United States.

3. Maine is the only state that shares its border with only one other state, New Hampshire.

4. Acadia National Park was the first national park east of the Mississippi River. Acadia National Park was established in 1919.

5. The state's official nickname is "Vacationland."

6. Maine's coastline is longer than California's when considering its many inlets and coves.

7. Portland, Maine, was named after the Isle of Portland in England.

8. Maine was initially part of Massachusetts until it gained statehood on March 15, 1820. Maine was the 23rd state admitted to the Union.

9. Lighthouses are an iconic feature of Maine's coastline, with over 60 still standing.

10. The Penobscot River is the longest river entirely in Maine.

11. Maine produces more blueberries than any other state in the U.S., accounting for over 90 percent of the blueberries produced in the United States.

12. The town of Eastport is the easternmost city in the United States.

13. The Appalachian Trail begins in Maine at Mount Katahdin, the tallest peak in the state.

14. Stephen King, the famous author, resides in Bangor, Maine, and many of his stories are set in the state.

15. The official state treat of Maine is the whoopie pie, a sweet dessert made from two cake-like cookies with a creamy filling.

16. Maine has the most prominent black bear population in the eastern United States.

17. The International Cryptozoology Museum in Portland is dedicated to the study of hidden or unknown animals.

18. The Sabbathday Lake Shaker Village in New Gloucester is the last active Shaker community.

19. Maine is home to over 6,000 lakes and ponds.

20. The state's official state soft drink is Moxie, a soft drink produced in Lowell, Massachusetts.

21. Maine's official state slogan is "The Way Life Should Be."

22. Maine has the highest moose population in the contiguous United States, with over 60,000 estimated moose calling it home.

23. The state flower of Maine isn't a flower, but rather the White pine cone and tassel.

24. Before becoming Maine's official state crustacean, lobsters were far from the delicacy they're considered today. Due to their plentiful availability, lobsters were utilized to feed prisoners and domestic workers, employed as crop fertilizer, or utilized as bait for capturing larger fish.

25. Maine has more than 4,000 islands.

26. The Desert of Maine is a 40-acre portion of Maine that is a desert.

27. Among all the states in the United States, Maine stands alone as the sole state whose name is a single syllable.

28. Maine is home to a size 410 boot that sits in front of the L.L. Bean flagship store.

29. Maine is home to Cadillac Mountain, the tallest mountain in the United States on the Atlantic Coast.

30. George Washington ordered the construction of Portland Head Light in Cape Elizabeth in 1791, prior to the formation of the U.S. government.

31. Maine gained statehood as part of the Missouri Compromise.

32. Maine has an umbrella cover museum with over 2,000 covers on display.

33. Maine sits at the 45th parallel, making it equidistant from the equator and the North Pole.

34. The town of Eastport is the first place in the United States to see the sunrise each morning.

35. Maine is responsible for around 40 million pounds of lobster each year, accounting for approximately 90 percent of the lobster in the United States.

36. Maine was home to the first naval battle of the Revolutionary War.

37. The area that is Agusta, Maine, Maine's capital, was initially explored by English settlers in 1607. The location wasn't settled until 1754, however.

38. The state bird of Maine is the black-capped chickadee.

39. The town of Bath holds the annual "Bath Heritage Days" festival, featuring the "Running of the Tub," where bathtubs are raced down the street.

40. The International Maritime Signal Flag "N" represents the letter "N" and stands for "no," which was adopted in recognition of Maine's "no" vote on prohibition.

41. Maine's unique coastline features more lighthouses on the Atlantic coast than any other state in the U.S.

42. The town of Eastport celebrates the "Great Sardine and Maple Leaf Drop" as part of its New Year's Eve festivities.

43. The Fryeburg Fair, one of Maine's largest agricultural fairs, attracts visitors with its "Largest Pumpkin" and "Largest Potato" contests.

44. Maine's official state cat, the Maine Coon cat, is known for its large size and tufted ears.

45. The North Atlantic right whale, one of the most endangered whale species, frequents the waters off the coast of Maine.

46. Maine's official state fish, the landlocked Atlantic salmon, is a unique species that spends its entire life in freshwater lakes.

47. Portland was the original capital of Maine until 1827, when it transferred to Agusta.

48. The "Annual Wife Carrying Championship" is held in Newry, where participants race while carrying their partners through an obstacle course.

49. John D. Rockefeller Jr. donated most of Acadia National Park's carriage roads and trail systems. The son of Standard Oil co-founder John D. Rockefeller donated over 50 miles of carriage trails to Acadia National Park.

50. Kennebunkport is also home to the Seashore Trolley Museum, the world's oldest and largest museum of mass transit.

MARYLAND

1. Maryland is known as the "Old Line State." A name given to the state by General George Washington.

2. The state's official nickname is also "The Free State," referring to Maryland's stance on religious freedom. The state also has the nicknames: "Little America" and "America in Miniature."

3. Maryland was one of the original 13 colonies that declared independence from British rule.

4. The U.S. Naval Academy is in Annapolis, training future Navy and Marine Corps officers.

5. The Chesapeake Bay is the largest estuary in the United States and a defining geographical feature of Maryland.

6. The Maryland Blue Crab is a symbol of the state and a culinary delight.

7. Maryland was the seventh state to ratify the U.S. Constitution in 1788.

8. The state is home to Fort McHenry, where Francis Scott Key wrote "The Star-Spangled Banner" lyrics during the War of 1812.

9. The Baltimore and Ohio Railroad, the oldest railroad in the U.S., began operations in Baltimore.

10. The Maryland Zoo in Baltimore is one of the oldest zoos in the United States and the third-largest in the United States.

11. The city of Cumberland is the western terminus of the Chesapeake and Ohio Canal.

12. Maryland was founded as a proprietary colony by Cecil Calvert, the second Lord Baltimore, in 1632.

13. Annapolis, the capital of Maine, was originally called Providence due to its original Puritan settlers.

14. The state's official sport is jousting, a medieval form of competition.

15. Maryland's flag is the only one based on English heraldry, combining the coats of arms of the Calvert and Crossland families.

16. The U.S. Census Bureau is headquartered in Suitland, Maryland.

17. Maryland is known for its crab feasts, where residents and visitors enjoy steamed crabs covered in Old Bay seasoning.

18. Maryland was the first state to designate a specific state exercise: walking.

19. The Ocean City Air Show features aerobatic performances over the ocean.

20. Maryland has five main geographical regions: Piedmont, Blue Ridge, Appalachian Valley, and Appalachian Plateau.

21. The city of Annapolis is home to the Maryland State House, the oldest state capitol still in continuous legislative use. The State House dates back to 1772.

22. The Havre de Grace Decoy Museum highlights the history of decoy carving.

23. Maryland has the highest average income of any state in the United States. Washington, D.C., a territory of the United States, is the only area with a higher median household income.

24. The "Oyster Wars" in the 19th century involved conflicts over oyster beds in Chesapeake Bay.

25. The Potomac River forms Maryland's border with Washington, D.C.

26. The Enoch Pratt Free Library in Baltimore was one of the first public library systems in the U.S. The library was founded in 1882.

27. The first dental school in the world, the Baltimore College of Dental Surgery, was established in Maryland in 1840.

28. *The Capital*, initially founded in 1884 as the *Evening Capital*, is one of the oldest newspapers in the United States.

29. The Great Baltimore Fire on February 8, 1904, gave way to national standards in firefighting equipment.

30. The "Poe Toaster" used to visit Edgar Allan Poe's grave in Baltimore every year on Poe's birthday, leaving behind a half-empty bottle of cognac and three roses.

31. Johns Hopkins University, founded in 1876, was the first university in the United States based on the European research institution model.

32. Edgar Allen Poe died in Baltimore a few days after being found delirious in the city's gutters.

33. The first telegraph message sent from Washington, D.C., was to Baltimore, and it read: "What hath God wrought?"

34. The Mountain Club of Maryland has placed painted green rocks along hiking trails, known as "trail magic," to guide hikers.

35. Maryland has a ghost story called the "Goatman," a half-man, half-goat creature rumored to live near Beltsville.

36. Accident, Maryland, was named after how it was discovered—by accident.

37. The National Historic Landmark Greenbelt community has streets named Crescent, Moonbeam, and UFO.

38. Maryland was named after Queen Henrietta Maria, the wife of King Charles I.

39. Assateague Island is known for its wild horses that inhabit the Island.

40. The Hell House Altar in Ellicott City has a tombstone-shaped altar believed to be cursed.

41. The Battle of Antietam in Sharpsburg, Maryland, on September 17, 1862, resulted in over 22,500 casualties between the Union and the Confederacy.

42. The Preakness Stakes, the second leg of the Triple Crown, is held at Pimlico Race Course in Baltimore, Maryland. The third and final leg is the Belmont Stakes at Belmont Park in Elmont, New York.

43. The National Cryptologic Museum in Annapolis Junction explores the history of cryptology and codebreaking.

44. The American Visionary Art Museum in Baltimore features works by self-taught artists.

45. Baltimore was first established as a port for shipping grain and tobacco.

46. Maryland's official state dog, the Chesapeake Bay Retriever, is a breed developed in the state.

47. The town of Taneytown hosts an annual Taneytown Joust Festival, celebrating the state's official sport.

48. Maryland's official state boat, the skipjack, is used for oyster dredging on the Chesapeake Bay.

49. The Hancock area of Maryland is less than two miles (3.2 kilometers) wide, sandwiched between Pennsylvania and West Virginia.

50. The city of Annapolis is home to the U.S. Sailboat Show, the oldest in-water sailboat show in the world.

MASSACHUSETTS

1. Massachusetts is known as the "Bay State" due to its extensive coastline along the Atlantic Ocean.

2. The state's capital and largest city is Boston.

3. Massachusetts is home to Harvard University, the oldest institution of higher education in the United States, founded in 1636.

4. The Cape Cod National Seashore preserves 40 miles of pristine coastline and is a popular tourist destination.

5. Plymouth Rock, located in Plymouth, is believed to be the spot where the Mayflower Pilgrims first landed in 1620.

6. Massachusetts played a crucial role in the American Revolution, with events like the Boston Tea Party in 1773.

7. Massachusetts was admitted to the Union on February 6, 1788, making it the 6th state.

8. The official state dessert of Massachusetts is the Boston cream pie.

9. Massachusetts was the first state to legalize gay marriage in 2004.

10. Walden Pond in Concord was made famous by author Henry David Thoreau's book "Walden."

11. The Boston Marathon, one of the world's oldest annual marathons, takes place on Patriots' Day.

12. The Freedom Trail in Boston is a 2.5-mile-long (4-kilometer-long) path that passes by 17 historical sites significant to the American Revolution.

13. The Pilgrims in Plymouth celebrated the first Thanksgiving in 1621.

14. Massachusetts is home to the oldest continuously operating public park in the United States, Boston Common.

15. The Salem Witch Trials occurred in 1692, leading to a significant historical event in the state's history.

16. The *Make Way for Ducklings* statues in Boston's Public Garden pay tribute to the beloved children's book by Robert McCloskey.

17. The official state dog of Massachusetts is the Boston Terrier.

18. The first American lighthouse, Boston Light, was built on Little Brewster Island in 1716.

19. Located inside Boston National Historical Park, The USS Constitution, a historic Navy ship, is the oldest commissioned warship afloat in the world and is nicknamed "Old Ironsides."

20. The Lizzie Borden House is a Bed and Breakfast Museum in Fall River. It is the former home of Lizzie Borden, a woman famously accused of murdering her father and stepmother in 1892 with an axe.

21. The Massachusetts State House in Boston features a distinctive golden dome.

22. The Basketball Hall of Fame is in Springfield, Massachusetts, honoring basketball players and contributors.

23. The Plimoth Patuxet in Plymouth is a living history museum that recreates the Pilgrims' settlement.

24. The "Mapparium" in Boston's Christian Science Center is a three-story-tall stained glass globe.

25. The Granite Railway in Quincy is considered the first commercial railroad in the United States.

26. The first public school in the United States was in Boston, Massachusetts, known as the Boston Latin School.

27. Massachusetts was the first state to establish a state police force in 1865.

28. The city of Lowell is known as the "Cradle of the American Industrial Revolution" for its historic textile mills.

29. The New Bedford Whaling Museum celebrates the city's history as a major whaling port.

30. Massachusetts has the third-highest population density of any U.S. state.

31. The Paul Revere House in Boston's North End is the oldest remaining structure in downtown Boston. The house was built around 1680.

32. The official state cookie of Massachusetts is the chocolate chip cookie.

33. The Sandwich Glass Museum in Sandwich showcases glassmaking history and exhibits.

34. The official state folk hero is Johnny Appleseed, whose real name is John Chapman.

35. The American Antiquarian Society in Worcester houses one of the largest collections of materials from the colonial era and early America. Having been founded in 1812, it is the oldest historical society in the United States that has a national focus.

36. The city of Beverly was home to the first cotton mill in the United States.

37. The House of the Seven Gables in Salem inspired Nathaniel Hawthorne's novel of the same name.

38. Fall River's Battleship Cove features the USS Massachusetts battleship and other naval vessels.

39. The city of Gloucester has a long history as a fishing port and is known for its iconic *Man at the Wheel* statue, officially known as the Gloucester Fisherman's Memorial.

40. Massachusetts was the first state to have compulsory education laws in the U.S.

41. The Massachusetts Historical Society is the oldest historical society in the United States.

42. The official state polka is the "Say Hello to Someone in Massachusetts Polka."

43. The Massachusetts Turnpike is one of the oldest toll highways in the United States.

44. The Bridge of Flowers in Shelburne Falls is a former trolley bridge transformed into a blooming garden.

45. Massachusetts has a variety of scenic islands, including Martha's Vineyard and Nantucket.

46. The Museum of Bad Art, currently in Boston, Massachusetts, celebrates art that's "too bad to be ignored" and has had multiple locations within the state.

47. The Paper House in Rockport is entirely made of paper, including the furniture.

48. The world's oldest weather station, the Blue Hill Meteorological Observatory, is in Milton.

49. Dogtown in Gloucester is an abandoned settlement with boulders engraved with mysterious messages.

50. Fenway Park in Boston is one of the oldest Major League Baseball stadiums still in use. The baseball stadium was built in 1912.

MICHIGAN

1. Michigan is known as the "Great Lakes State" due to its proximity to four of the five Great Lakes: Superior, Michigan, Huron, and Erie.

2. The state's capital is Lansing, but its largest city is Detroit.

3. The Mackinac Bridge, connecting Michigan's Upper and Lower Peninsulas, is one of the longest suspension bridges in the world and the longest in the Western Hemisphere.

4. The world's first mile of concrete highway was Woodward Avenue in Detroit, Michigan, in 1909.

5. The Detroit River International Wildlife Refuge is North America's only international wildlife refuge.

6. Michigan is known for its extensive sand dunes, notably at Sleeping Bear Dunes National Lakeshore.

7. The Kellogg Company, famous for its breakfast cereals, was founded in Battle Creek, Michigan.

8. The Detroit Institute of Arts is home to one of the largest and most significant art collections in the United States.

9. Michigan has the longest freshwater coastline of any state in the United States.

10. Michigan is home to the world's largest limestone quarry in Rogers City.

11. The Heidelberg Project in Detroit is an outdoor art environment that transforms abandoned houses into vibrant installations.

12. The Detroit Zoo was the first zoo in the United States to use bar-less habitats.

13. Michigan has over 11,000 inland lakes, making it a popular destination for water recreation.

14. The Motown Museum in Detroit celebrates the history of Motown music.

15. Michigan is known for its production of cherries, particularly in the Traverse City area.

16. Michigan State University's "Beaumont Tower" in East Lansing chimes the alma mater daily.

17. Michigan has over 3,200 miles of shoreline along the Great Lakes.

18. The Kalamazoo Air Zoo Aerospace & Science Museum is an aviation museum and indoor amusement park.

19. Michigan is home to the International Cherry Pit-Spitting Championship at Tree-Mendus Fruit Farm in Eau Claire.

20. The Charles H. Wright Museum of African-American History in Detroit is one of the most prominent African-American museums in the world.

21. Michigan State University was The first university to teach scientific agriculture in the United States in 1857.

22. Michigan's state motto is "Si quaeris peninsulamamoenam circumspice," Latin for "If you seek a pleasant peninsula, look about you."

23. Michigan's Upper Peninsula (UP) is often affectionately called "Yooper" territory, with a distinct regional culture.

24. Detroit is known as the "Motor City" due to its historical significance in the automobile industry.

25. Michigan is home to the only "Floating Post Office" in the United States. The post office serves residents of Mackinac Island.

26. The state's official state flower is the apple blossom.

27. The U.S. National Geographic Traveler named the Sleeping Bear Dunes on Lake Michigan "The Most Beautiful Place in America."

28. Although Michigan does not border an ocean, the state has more than 120 lighthouses dotting its shores.

29. The city of Holland hosts the annual Tulip Time Festival, celebrating Dutch heritage.

30. Michigan's state fossil is the mastodon.

31. Sault Ste. Marie, Michigan, is located in the Upper Peninsula and was settled in 1668, making it the oldest city in Michigan.

32. The city of Frankenmuth is known as "Little Bavaria" and is famous for its German-style architecture and traditions.

33. No point in Michigan is further than 85 miles (136 kilometers) from one of the Great Lakes.

34. The city of Marquette has an annual U.P. 200 Sled Dog Championship, showcasing sled dog racing.

35. The Greenfield Village in Dearborn is an open-air museum that showcases historic buildings and exhibits.

36. Oval Beach in Saugatuck has been named one of the best beaches in the U.S.

37. The city of Detroit has a vibrant arts and music scene, with Motown Records originating there.

38. Michigan has over 400 named islands.

39. The Frankenmuth Brewery is Michigan's oldest microbrewery, operating since 1862.

40. Michigan is home to the Saugatuck Chain Ferry, Diane, the last remaining hand-cranked chain ferry in the United States. Diane crosses the Kalamazoo River.

41. The city of Traverse City is known as the "Cherry Capital of the World."

42. The Arab American National Museum in Dearborn celebrates the history and contributions of Arab Americans.

43. The city of Battle Creek is known for its annual Cereal Festival, celebrating its history as the cereal capital.

44. Hell is a township in Michigan without defined boundaries or population statistics.

45. The House of David in Benton Harbor once fielded a baseball team known for their long beards and unique plays.

46. The city of Frankenmuth is known for having the world's largest Christmas store, Bronner's Christmas Wonderland.

47. The Mystery Spot in St. Ignace claims to be a gravitational anomaly, causing objects to appear to defy the laws of physics.

48. Little Caesars Pizza was founded by Mike and Marian Ilitch in Garden City, Michigan, in 1959.

49. In 1938, a group of pranksters stole the "M" from the University of Michigan's iconic "Michigan Stadium" scoreboard, which read "ICHIGAN."

50. Michigan has its own "Stonehenge-like" structure that exists below the surface of Lake Michigan and is believed to be around 9,000 years old.

MINNESOTA

1. Minnesota is known as the "Land of 10,000 Lakes," but it actually has more than 11,000 lakes.

2. The state's capital is St. Paul, and its largest city is Minneapolis.

3. The Mall of America in Bloomington is the largest shopping mall in the United States.

4. The official state flower of Minnesota is the lady's slipper, specifically the pink and white lady's slipper.

5. Minnesota is home to Split Rock Lighthouse, which sits on Lake Superior's rugged North Shore and is considered one of the most picturesque lighthouses in the United States.

6. Minnesota is known for its Scandinavian heritage, with strong ties to countries like Norway and Sweden.

7. The Great Minnesota Get-Together refers to the Minnesota State Fair, one of the largest state fairs in the United States.

8. On May 11, 1858, Minnesota became the 32nd state to join the Union.

9. The Jolly Green Giant statue in Blue Earth pays homage to the brand's famous mascot.

10. Lake Itasca in Itasca State Park is the headwaters of the Mississippi River.

11. The Mill City Museum in Minneapolis showcases the city's history as a flour milling capital.

12. The state's official muffin is the blueberry muffin.

13. Minnesota is home to the world's largest pelican statue, located in Pelican Rapids.

14. The Paul and Babe statues in Bemidji pay tribute to Paul Bunyan and his blue ox, Babe.

15. The International Wolf Center in Ely educates visitors about wolves and their role in ecosystems.

16. Minnesota is known for its diverse cuisine, including dishes like hot dish, wild rice soup, and lutefisk.

17. The two largest cities in Minnesota are Minneapolis and Saint Paul. Due to their proximity to each other, they are known as the "Twin Cities."

18. The state is known for its unique Juicy Lucy burger, which has cheese stuffed inside the patty.

19. The International Owl Center in Houston, Minnesota, is dedicated to the study and appreciation of owls.

20. The SPAM Museum in Austin, Minnesota, celebrates the history of the canned meat product.

21. Minneapolis holds an annual Art Sled Rally, where people race creatively decorated sleds down a hill.

22. The name "Minnesota" comes from the Sioux words "minni" and "sotah," which translates to "sky-tinted water" or "cloudy water."

23. Minnesota's Skyway System' in Minneapolis, spanning over 11 miles, allows pedestrians to navigate the city without going outdoors during cold weather.

24. The Big Ole statue in Alexandria, Minnesota, depicts a Viking holding a shield. The statue was built in 1965 and stands 28 feet (8.5 meters) tall.

25. The Pine City Pioneer statue in Pine City commemorates the giant pine trees that were once abundant in the area. The redwood was carved by chainsaw and is 35 feet (10.7 meters) tall.

26. The Dala Horse statue in Mora, Minnesota, pays homage to the Swedish heritage of the area. The horse is 22 feet (6.7 meters) tall.

27. The "World's Largest Free-Standing Hockey Stick and Puck" can be found in Eveleth, Minnesota, coming in at 110 feet (33.5 meters) tall and over 700 pounds (317 kilograms).

28. The Mayo Clinic was founded in Rochester, Minnesota, in 1864 and is regarded as one of the top medical centers in the world.

29. Eagle Mountain is the highest point in Minnesota at 2,301 feet (701 meters) above sea level.

30. The Minnesota State Capitol in St. Paul has a golden chariot on its rooftop called the Quadriga.

31. "Lake Wobegon" from Garrison Keillor's radio show *A Prairie Home Companion*, is a fictional town in Minnesota.

32. Meat Raffles are a unique Minnesota tradition where meat is raffled off in bars and restaurants.

33 Minnesota's Pumpkin Regatta involves racing across a lake in giant, hollowed-out pumpkins.

34. The movie *Fargo* was filmed mainly in Minnesota, even though the story is set in North Dakota.

35. The Palmer House Hotel in Sauk Centre, Minnesota, was the first building in the city to have electricity.

36. Minnesota was home to the country's largest mass execution in 1962 when 38 Sioux men were hanged.

37. Minnesota has no rivers that flow into the state; it is upstream of every U.S. river.

38. Certain items, those considered a necessity, do not have sales tax in Minnesota.

39. Minnesota has around 2,700 wolves, which accounts for nearly half of all wolves in the lower 48 states.

40. Minnesota is the northernmost state among the contiguous Lower 48 states and uniquely possesses a land area north of the 49th parallel known as the Northwest Angle. This isolated region is physically disconnected from the rest of the United States.

41. Minnesota has the largest Somali population outside of Africa.

42. The Mississippi River, the Red River of the North, and the St. Louis River all originate in Minnesota, making it the only state that is the source of three major rivers.

43. St. Paul, Minnesota, was once known as "Pig's Eye."

44. Minnesota was carved out by glaciers in the last ice age.

45. Minnesota has 11 federally recognized American Indian tribes.

46. Part of Minnesota requires driving through Canada to get to.

47. Minnesota is responsible for more turkeys than any other state.

48. The first intercollegiate basketball game took place in Minnesota in 1895. The final score of the game was 9-3.

49. The Metrodome in Minneapolis is the only stadium to host an NCAA Final Four Basketball Championship, A World Series, and a Super Bowl.

50. Minneapolis experiences an average of 20 sub-zero days each year, making it the coldest major city in the U.S.

MISSISSIPPI

1. Mississippi is known as the "Magnolia State."

2. The state's capital is Jackson, its largest city.

3. Mississippi is named after the Mississippi River, which flows along its western boundary.

4. The official state flower of Mississippi is the magnolia.

5. The Natchez Trace Parkway is a historic scenic road running from Natchez, Mississippi, to Nashville, Tennessee.

6. The Mississippi River is the second-longest river in North America, and it forms the state's western border.

7. Mississippi is known for its rich blues music heritage.

8. Elvis Presley was born in Tupelo, Mississippi.

9. The Biloxi Lighthouse, first lit in 1848, is one of the oldest lighthouses in the United States.

10. The Vicksburg National Cemetery is the final resting place of around 17,0000 Civil War soldiers.

11. Mississippi is one of the country's leading producers of farm-raised catfish.

12. The Tupelo Buffalo Park and Zoo is home to a variety of animals and a large buffalo herd.

13. Mississippi has diverse ecosystems, from forests and wetlands to coastal areas.

14. Mississippi is known for its iconic Southern dishes like grits and fried chicken.

15. The Mississippi Petrified Forest near Flora features ancient petrified wood.

16. Mississippi has a rich gospel music tradition, with many churches and events.

17. The state is home to the International Checkers Hall of Fame.

18. The first lung transplant in the world was performed at the University Hospital in Jackson, Mississippi.

19. Mississippi has a town called Hot Coffee, located in the southern part of the state.

20. Leland, Mississippi, is home to the Birthplace of Kermit the Frog Museum.

21. Mississippi is the most recent state to add lotto games; it did so in 2019, making buying a lotto ticket in Mississippi now legal.

22. The state's official toy is the Teddy Bear.

23. In Mississippi, it is illegal to explain what polygamy is.

24. Profanity in public is not allowed, and you could be fined for cursing in public in Mississippi.

25. Mississippi was the last state to ratify the 13th Amendment, abolishing slavery; it finally submitted the required documentation on February 7, 2013.

26. Mississippi was the first state to ratify the 18th Amendment, which initiated Prohibition.

27. The state's official reptile is the American alligator.

28. In Biloxi, there's a historic house, the Old Brick House, that has withstood hurricanes, fires, and even Civil War cannonballs.

29. Mississippi is strongly associated with sweet tea, often called the "House Wine of the South."

30. The Mississippi Petrified Forest is one of the few places you can see petrified logs still in the ground.

31. The Mississippi State Capitol's dome is the third-tallest in the United States. The dome reaches a height of 180 feet (54.9 meters).

32. Biloxi, Mississippi, is known as the original "Seafood Capital of the World."

33. In Mississippi, the Natchez Under-the-Hill Saloon once hosted riverboat gamblers and pirates.

34. Mississippi has a Tamale Trail celebrating the state's tamale-making tradition.

35. The Winterville Mounds are one of the most significant prehistoric mound complexes in the United States.

36. Mississippi's capital, Jackson, was named after President Andrew Jackson.

37. The John C. Stennis Space Center in Hancock County is NASA's largest rocket engine testing facility.

38. Mississippi's motto, "Virtute et armis," translates to "By Valor and Arms."

39. The Mississippi Watermelon Festival in Mize, Mississippi, includes seed-spitting contests and watermelon-shaped floats.

40. The World Catfish Festival in Belzoni includes events like hog calling and a catfish toss.

41. The Biedenharn Coca-Cola Museum in Vicksburg was the first place to bottle Coca-Cola. The bottling was done in 1894 at the Biedenharn Candy Company.

42. The John C. Stennis Lock and Dam on the Tennessee-Tombigbee Waterway is one of the largest locks in the U.S.

43. Mississippi's official "Bicentennial Quilt" features designs from all 82 counties.

44. The Mississippi State Fair covers over 100 acres (40 hectares).

45. Mississippi's name comes from the Chippewa Indians, meaning "large river."

46. Mississippi has had three different state flags, with the current version being adopted in 2020.

47. The average elevation of Mississippi is only 300 feet (91.4 meters) above sea level.

48. There is an average of one church, temple, or other place of worship per every 270 residents of the state.

49. The first settlers of Mississippi were French.

50. The highest point in Mississippi is Woodall Mountain, with an elevation of 806 feet (244.7 meters).

MISSOURI

1. Missouri is known as the "Show-Me State."

2. The state's capital is Jefferson City.

3. The Gateway Arch in St. Louis is a famous symbol of the city and the state.

4. Missouri is bordered by eight states: Iowa, Illinois, Kentucky, Tennessee, Arkansas, Oklahoma, Kansas, and Nebraska.

5. The Mississippi River creates Missouri's eastern border.

6. The Anheuser-Busch Brewery in St. Louis is one of the largest beer producers in the world.

7. Missouri's official state bird is the eastern bluebird.

8. The Missouri River is the longest river in North America.

9. The state's official motto is "Salus populi suprema lex esto," meaning "Let the welfare of the people be the supreme law."

10. The St. Louis Zoo is one of the oldest zoos in the United States.

11. The Mark Twain Boyhood Home and Museum in Hannibal celebrates the famous author's life.

12. Missouri is often associated with the "Gateway to the West" due to its historical role in westward expansion.

13. The state's official musical instrument is the fiddle.

14. Missouri is known for its unique regional dialect, often called "the Missouri accent."

15. The Wilson's Creek National Battlefield commemorates a Civil War battle near Springfield, the first major battle fought west of the Mississippi River.

16. The Budweiser Clydesdales, a team of iconic horses, are based in St. Louis.

17. In 2008, the state's official dessert became the ice cream cone, a nod to the 1904 St. Louis World Fair.

18. The Pony Express National Museum in St. Joseph explores the history of the Pony Express mail service.

19. Missouri is home to the Kansas City Art Institute and the St. Louis Art Museum.

20. Missouri's Silver Dollar City is a popular theme park near Branson.

21. The Museum of Westward Expansion is located beneath the Gateway Arch.

22. Missouri's Whiteman Air Force Base is home to the B-2 Spirit stealth bomber.

23. The Jesse James Home Museum in St. Joseph is the house where the infamous outlaw was killed.

24. The National Tiger Sanctuary in Saddlebrooke provides a safe haven for rescued big cats.

25. The Muny in St. Louis is the largest and oldest outdoor musical theater in the United States.

26. The Battle of Carthage State Historic Site preserves a site from the Civil War's Battle of Carthage.

27. The National Churchill Museum in Fulton honors Winston Churchill and features a section of the Berlin Wall.

28. The Elephant Rocks State Park in Bellview, Missouri, features giant granite boulders that resemble a train of elephants.

29. Missouri is known for its abundance of caves, including the famous Meramec Caverns.

30. The Ozark National Scenic Riverways is the first national park area to protect a river system.

31. The World Bird Sanctuary in Valley Park is dedicated to the conservation of birds of prey.

32. Missouri's Perry County Circuit Courthouse in Perryville is one of the oldest active courthouse west of the Mississippi River. The courthouse was built in 1821.

33. The Laura Ingalls Wilder Home and Museum in Mansfield celebrates the author of the *Little House on the Prairie* series.

34. Missouri's state aquatic animal is the paddlefish.

35. Missouri has a rich history of steamboat travel on its rivers.

36. The Graham Cave State Park contains archaeological evidence of prehistoric Native American habitation.

37. The St. Louis Walk of Fame in the Delmar Loop honors notable St. Louisans.

38. The Butterfly House in Chesterfield features a conservatory filled with butterflies.

39. The St. Louis Mercantile Library is the oldest library west of the Mississippi River.

40. The National Geospatial-Intelligence Agency (NGA) operates a major facility in St. Louis. The agency plays a vital role in national security.

41. The Gateway Arch in St. Louis is the tallest national monument in the United States. The Arch measures 305 feet (93 meters) tall and was a gift from France in 1885.

42. Missouri has a town named Tightwad, known for its frugality.

43. The town of Uranus, Missouri, is home to a Fudge Factory and General Store. The town is found along the former U.S. Route 66.

44. The Walt Disney Hometown Museum in Marceline celebrates the life of the famous animator.

45. Missouri has a town named Humansville. The population of Humansville is just under 1,000.

46. Missouri is known for the "St. Louis Gooey Butter Cake," a unique and delicious dessert.

47. Kansas City is split, with half being in Missouri and the other half in Kansas because Kansas did not exist when it was settled.

48. The state flag of Missouri features two grizzly bears; however, grizzly bears have never lived in Missouri as the climate is not ideal for their survival.

49. The Gateway Arch is the smallest national park in the United States at only 192 acres (77.7 hectares).

50. Saint Louis University was the first university west of the Mississippi, opening its doors in 1832.

MONTANA

1. Montana is known as the "Treasure State."

2. The state's capital is Helena.

3. Montana is the fourth largest state in the United States.

4. The state's nickname, "Big Sky Country," reflects its expansive skies.

5. Montana is home to Glacier National Park, known as the "Crown of the Continent."

6. Yellowstone National Park, the first national park in the world, spans Montana and Wyoming.

7. The Missouri River flows through Montana.

8. The state's official flower is the bitterroot.

9. The Little Bighorn Battlefield National Monument in Crow Agency, Montana, commemorates the Battle of the Little Bighorn.

10. The Yellowstone River is one of the longest free-flowing rivers in the United States and flows mainly through Montana.

11. Montana's state fish is the Westslope cutthroat trout.

12. Montana is home to the World Museum of Mining in Butte.

13. Montana's official state mammal is the grizzly bear.

14. The state's official song is "Montana."

15. Montana's Makoshika State Park is the largest state park in Montana and contains badlands formations.

16. Montana is known for its abundance of wildlife, including elk, bison, and wolves.

17. The Pompeys Pillar National Monument features the only physical evidence of the Lewis and Clark Expedition, an inscription left by William Clark.

18. The National Bison Range is home to one of the oldest bison herds in the United States and was established in 1908.

19. Montana's Flathead Lake is the largest natural freshwater lake west of the Mississippi River.

20. Montana has a relatively low population density, contributing to its wide open spaces.

21. Montana joined the Union on November 8, 1889, making it the 41st state.

22. Montana's Pictograph Cave State Park contains ancient rock art from over 2,000 years ago.

23. The Old Prison Museum in Deer Lodge is a former state prison that offers guided tours.

24. Montana's Marias River Massacre Site commemorates a tragic conflict between the U.S. Army and Blackfeet Indians.

25. The Museum of Mountain Flying in Missoula highlights the history of aviation in mountainous regions.

26. Montana's Wild Horse Island State Park in Lake County, Montana, is home to wild horses and other wildlife.

27. Montana's official state microbe is Saccharomyces cerevisiae, a yeast used in bread and beer production. The yeast is the determining factor between whether the beer will be an ale or a lager. The yeast produces an ale, while lagers are fermented with Saccharomyces pastorianus.

28. The Ringing Rocks in Butte are a unique geological phenomenon where rocks create musical tones when struck.

29. Montana's state motto is "Oro y Plata," meaning "Gold and Silver."

30. The Two Medicine Dinosaur Center in Bynum features a paleontology museum and guided dinosaur digs.

31. Montana's First Peoples Buffalo Jump State Park preserves a historic Native American buffalo hunting site.

32. Montana's Pompeys Pillar National Monument is named after Sacagawea's son, Pomp.

33. Ted Turner, the founder of TNT, TBS, and CNN, owns 148,870 acres (60,245 hectares) of land in Montana, making him only the 9th largest private landowner in the state.

34. The World Famous Sip 'n Dip Lounge in Great Falls features live mermaid performances in its pool.

35. The National Bison Range was established after President Roosevelt bought a bison herd for his personal ranch.

36. Montana's Jim's Horn House in Three Forks, Montana, features a collection of over 2,000 animal horns.

37. Montana's Museum of the Rockies has a "World's Largest T-Rex Skull" on display.

38. Shelby, Montana, was the site of the 1923 World Championship boxing match between Jack Dempsey and Tommy Gibbons.

39. Montana is home to the world's shortest river, the Roe River, flowing only 201 feet (61 meters).

40. The Church of Jesus Christ of Latter-Day Saints owns 151,840 acres (61,447 hectares) in the state.

41. Montana shares an international border with three Canadian provinces: British Columbia, Alberta, and Saskatchewan. No other state has as many international borders.

42. Loma, Montana, once experienced a world record 54-degree temperature change in 24 hours, with the temperature ranging from 49 to 103 degrees.

43. Montana is home to Beaver Creek Park. At 10,000 acres (4,047 hectares), it is the largest country park in the country.

44. Water from snow melt in Montana reaches the Pacific, Atlantic, and Southern oceans.

45. Billings, Montana, has over 115,000 residents, making it the only city in the state with more than 100,000 residents. The next highest city is Missoula, coming in at just under 77,000.

46. The name Montana comes from the Spanish montaña, meaning mountain.

47. Although the name is derived from Spanish, the first settlers of Montana were French.

48. Twenty-four different Native American tribes were once within Montana's borders.

49. Bannack, Montana's first capital, is now a ghost town, with the last residents leaving in the 1970s.

50. Montana was the first state to elect a woman to Congress when it elected Jeannette Rankin in 1916.

NEBRASKA

1. Nebraska is known as the "Cornhusker State."

2. The Sandhills region of Nebraska contains the largest area of stabilized sand dunes in the Western Hemisphere.

3. Nebraska's official state flower is the tall goldenrod.

4. Omaha's Henry Doorly Zoo and Aquarium is consistently ranked as one of the best zoos in the world.

5. Kool-Aid was invented in Hastings, Nebraska, by Edwin Perkins.

6. The Arbor Lodge State Historical Park in Nebraska City was the former residence of J. Sterling Morton, the founder of Arbor Day.

7. The Chimney Rock National Historic Site was a prominent landmark for pioneers traveling on the Oregon Trail. The peak of the rock is 4,228 feet (1,288.7 meters) above sea level.

8. The state is home to the Great Platte River Road Archway Monument, a unique museum spanning Interstate 80.

9. The Toadstool Geologic Park in the Oglala National Grassland features unique rock formations.

10. The Golden Spike Tower in North Platte offers views of Union Pacific's Bailey Yard, the largest rail yard in the world.

11. The Lied Jungle at Omaha's Henry Doorly Zoo is the largest indoor rainforest in the United States.

12. The Ogallala Aquifer, located beneath Nebraska, is one of the world's largest underground sources of freshwater.

13. The Crane Trust Nature and Visitor Center near Grand Island offers views of sandhill cranes during migration.

14. The John C. Fremont Days Festival in Fremont celebrates the life and accomplishments of explorer John C. Fremont.

15. The Buffalo Bill Ranch State Historical Park in North Platte was the former home of Buffalo Bill Cody.

16. Nebraska's state mammal, the white-tailed deer, is commonly found throughout the state.

17. Nebraska's Czech Festival in Wilber celebrates Czech heritage with food, music, and dancing.

18. Nebraska's Seward Fourth of July Celebration is one of the nation's oldest and largest Independence Day events.

19. The Nebraska National Forest and Charles E. Bessey Tree Nursery was established in 1902 near Halsey, Nebraska, and is the largest hand-planted forest in the United States.

20. Nebraska was once called the "Tree Planters' State" due to its emphasis on reforestation efforts.

21. The town of Alliance is home to Carhenge, a replica of Stonehenge made from vintage cars.

22. Hastings, Nebraska, has a Kool-Aid Day festival to honor the drink's inventor, Edwin Perkins.

23. In 2021, the 100-millionth tree was planted in Nebraska.

24. Nebraska joined the Union on March 1, 1867. Nebraska was the 37th state to do so.

25. Nebraska is home to more than 75,000 miles (120,700 kilometers) of riverways.

26. Nebraska's state capital is designed in the style of Art Deco.

27. The University of Nebraska Cornhuskers football stadium holds more than 90,000 people, a number that is more than any professional sports stadium in the United States.

28. Until 1762, Nebraska was part of French Louisiana.

29. Nebraska is home to a porch swing that is 32 feet (9.75 meters) long. The swing can fit 18 adults.

30. The Museum of Shadows, located in Omaha, is a haven for enthusiasts of the eerie and mysterious. Within its walls, you'll find a staggering assemblage of 3,000 items that have undergone certification for being haunted. This quantity establishes a record-breaking compilation of haunted relics on a global scale.

31. The Reuben sandwich was invented in Omaha, Nebraska, in 1925 by Reuben Kulakofsky.

32. Only around eight percent of Nebraska is not farmland or ranchland.

33. Omaha was the capital of Nebraska until 1854.

34. The Nebraska State Capitol in Lincoln is the second tallest in the United States, standing 400 feet (122 meters) tall.

35. Nebraska has a town named Valentine that receives thousands of cards around the Valentine's Day holiday.

36. The uniqueness of Nebraska's Legislature lies in its singular structure within the United States. It stands as the lone legislative body with a unicameral system, denoting the presence of a single house. What sets it apart further is that its members are elected without party affiliation.

37. Omaha was the starting point of the first railroad line that went to the Pacific Coast.

38. Although Nebraska is landlocked, the state has its own navy.

39. In 1986, a historic occurrence took place in Nebraska when, for the very first time, two women competed against each other in the race to govern a state.

40. Nebraska is home to a statue of Chef Boyardee. The bronze statue of Chef Hector Boiardi was unveiled to commemorate the 90th anniversary of the brand.

41. Maskell City Hall is the smallest city hall in the United States, measuring 10 x 12 feet (3 x 3.66 meters).

42. On average, it is estimated that there are at least ten ancient elephant remains per square mile interred within the soil of Nebraska.

43. Monowi, Nebraska, has a population of one.

44. Nebraska was bombed by the Japanese during World War II.

45. Nebraska is triply landlocked, which requires traveling through at least three states to reach any gulf, ocean, or bay. It is the only state with this distinction.

46. The world's largest stamp ball can be found in Boys Town, Nebraska. Created with canceled stamps, the ball weighs around 600 pounds (272 kilograms).

47. You can find the largest collection of roller skating artifacts and textual materials in the world at the National Museum of Roller Skating in Lincoln.

48. The ski lift was invented in Nebraska.

49. The TV dinner originated in Nebraska thanks to Gilbert and Clarke Swanson; their products can still be found today.

50. At one point, the town of Lehigh had banned the sale of doughnut holes.

NEVADA

1. Nevada is known as the "Silver State" due to its historical silver mining industry.

2. The state's capital is Carson City, while its largest city is Las Vegas.

3. Nevada is the only U.S. state where prostitution is legal in some counties.

4. The famous Las Vegas Strip is home to some of the world's largest hotels and casinos.

5. The Hoover Dam, located on the border of Nevada and Arizona, is one of the world's engineering marvels.

6. The Welcome to Fabulous Las Vegas sign is an iconic landmark on the Las Vegas Strip.

7. Nevada is the driest state in the U.S., with an average annual rainfall of about seven inches.

8. Area 51, a highly secretive U.S. military facility, is in Nevada's desert.

9. The state's nickname "Battle Born" refers to its admission to the Union during the Civil War.

10. Nevada's Great Basin National Park features the Lehman Caves, a system of beautiful underground caves.

11. The Black Rock Desert is home to the annual Burning Man festival, attracting thousands of participants.

12. Lake Tahoe, which straddles the Nevada-California border, is the largest alpine lake in North America.

13. The "Loneliest Road in America," U.S. Route 50, passes through Nevada's vast desert regions.

14. Nevada's Valley of Fire State Park is known for its vibrant red sandstone formations.

15. Reno, known as the "Biggest Little City in the World," is famous for its casinos and entertainment. The city is also home to the University of Nevada, Reno.

16. The official state colors of Nevada are silver and blue, as designated by Nevada Revised Statute 235.025.

17. The Nevada Test Site, north of Las Vegas, was a major location for nuclear weapons testing during the Cold War.

18. The state is home to various desert wildlife, including rattlesnakes, coyotes, and jackrabbits.

19. Nevada has more hotel rooms per capita than any other state.

20. The Berlin-Ichthyosaur State Park in Austin, Nevada, features well-preserved ichthyosaur fossils.

21. Lake Mead, formed by the Hoover Dam, is the largest reservoir in the U.S. by volume.

22. Nevada is one of the few states without a state income tax.

23. The Great Basin is a vast region of deserts, mountains, and valleys in Nevada.

24. Nevada's state flower is the sagebrush, a common desert shrub.

25. Virginia City, a historic mining town, played a significant role during the Comstock Lode silver rush.

26. The "E.T. Highway" in Nevada is famous for its extraterrestrial-themed attractions and proximity to Area 51.

27. The state's highest point is Boundary Peak, reaching 13,147 feet (3,977 meters).

28. The Ruby Mountains are known for their stunning alpine scenery and wildlife.

29. Nevada is home to numerous ghost towns, remnants of its mining boom era.

30. The Ward Charcoal Ovens State Historic Park in White Pine County, Nevada, features beehive-shaped charcoal kilns that operated from 1876 to 1879.

31. The Red Rock Canyon National Conservation Area near Las Vegas features stunning red rock formations.

32. Nevada's state fish is the Lahontan cutthroat trout, a large and ancient species.

33. The Old Las Vegas Mormon Fort State Historic Park is the site of the first permanent non-native settlement in the Las Vegas Valley.

34. Nevada's state animal is the desert bighorn sheep.

35. Nevada has the third largest Basque population in the United States, primarily residing in the town of Winnemucca.

36. Every January, the town of Elko hosts the National Cowboy Poetry Gathering, celebrating the art of cowboy poetry and storytelling.

37. Nevada has a state rifle, the Winchester Model 1873.

38. Although Nevada is the 7th largest state in terms of land area, 89 percent of the state's population lives in either the Las Vegas or Reno metro areas.

39. There are around 800 wild horses in Nevada.

40. Thousands of classic cars and music enthusiasts gather in Reno during Hot August Nights to celebrate classic cars, rock 'n' roll, and nostalgia.

41. In the early 20th century, Nevada gained a reputation as the "Divorce Capital of the World" due to its lenient divorce laws, allowing couples to establish residency quickly for divorce proceedings.

42. Nevada boasts more mountain ranges than any other state in the U.S.

43. Marion Motley, one of the first two African Americans to play professional football, played for the University of Nevada Wolf Pack in Reno.

44. Nevada has the fifth-highest Mormon population outside of Utah, with over 180,000 people identifying as Mormon.

45. Boulder City, located near Hoover Dam, was originally established as a federal construction camp and prohibited alcohol until 1969.

46. Lake Tahoe's water is known for its remarkable clarity, allowing for visibility up to 70 feet (21 meters) deep.

47. Blue Jeans were invented in Reno by Jacob Davis, a tailor, in 1870. Jacob Davis later partnered with Levi Strauss.

48. Las Vegas sits 2,001 feet (610 meters) above sea level.

49. Boulder City is one of only two places in Nevada where gambling is prohibited. The other is Panaca.

50. Lake Tahoe is the second deepest lake in the United States, with a depth of 1,645 feet (501 meters).

O. Michael Maysam

NEW HAMPSHIRE

1. New Hampshire's state motto, "Live free or die," reflects its independent spirit.

2. New Hampshire is often called the "Granite State" due to its abundant granite deposits and historical quarrying.

3. The New Hampshire primary is famous for being the first primary in the U.S. presidential election cycle.

4. Mount Washington's summit is known for its extreme weather and strong winds, which once held the world's highest wind speed record.

5. The famous Old Man of the Mountain rock formation on Cannon Mountain collapsed in 2003.

6. New Hampshire has only 18 miles of coastline, but it's known for its picturesque beaches and historic towns.

7. New Hampshire has no state sales tax, making it a shopping destination for neighboring states.

8. There is no mandatory seatbelt law for adults in New Hampshire.

9. Laconia hosts the annual New Hampshire Pumpkin Festival, where thousands of carved pumpkins illuminate the city.

10. Salem is home to "America's Stonehenge," a mysterious archaeological site with stone structures.

11. New Hampshire produces high-quality maple syrup during the sugaring season.

12. New Hampshire is known for its accessible voting laws and same-day voter registration.

13. The Isle of Shoals, located off the coast, is known for its history and haunting tales.

14. The Exeter UFO Festival celebrates the town's history of UFO sightings.

15. Crotched Mountain offers night skiing under the lights.

16. Wolfeboro claims to be America's "Oldest Summer Resort Town."

17. New Hampshire is known for its apple orchards and cider.

18. Portsmouth is home to the USS Albacore submarine museum.

19. Funspot Arcade in Laconia is the largest arcades in the world.

20. Alton Bay on Lake Winnipesaukee has an ice runway for small planes during the winter.

21. The Porcupine Freedom Festival in Lancaster, also known as PorcFest, celebrates personal and economic freedom and has been held every June for the last 19 years.

22. The New Hampshire Highland Games in Lincoln, New Hampshire, celebrate Scottish heritage.

23. Endicott Rock in Weirs Beach bears inscriptions dating back to 1652.

24. Mount Washington is home to the second-highest wind speed ever officially recorded. On April 12, 1934, wind speeds reached 231 miles per hour (371 kilometers per hour); the fastest wind speed ever recorded was on Barrow Island, Australia, when it reached 253 miles per hour (408kilometers per hour) on April 10, 1996.

25. Chutters Candy Store in Littleton is home to the world's longest candy counter at 112 feet (34 meters) long.

26. New Hampshire was the 9th state to join the Union. It did so on June 21, 1788.

27. Founded in 1916, Laconia hosts one of the oldest motorcycle rallies in the U.S., Laconia Motorcycle Week.

28. New Hampshire's Route 4 is known as "Antique Alley" for its many antique shops.

29. Bedell Bridge State Historic Site features the remnants of the historic Bedell Bridge, which was destroyed by wind in 1979. The bridge was the second-longest covered bridge in the United States.

30. New Hampshire offers moose-watching tours.

31. The Madison Boulder is the largest glacial erratic (a glacially deposited rock) in North America, weighing around 5,000 tons.

32. Frankenstein Cliff in Crawford Notch was named after early explorers who believed the rock formations resembled the monster.

33. New Hampshire prohibits requiring a blood test for marriage licenses.

34. The movie *On Golden Pond* was filmed on Squam Lake, and the town of Holderness hosts an annual Squam Lakes Film Festival.

35. Route 3 in Pittsburg, New Hampshire, is known as "Moose Alley" for frequent moose sightings.

36. The Cheshire Children's Museum in Keene prides itself on interactive exhibits, including a human hamster wheel.

37. New Hampshire's "Moose Plate" program supports wildlife conservation and features a moose emblem on license plates.

38. The first potato planted in the United States was brought from Derry, Northern Ireland, and was planted in New Hampshire.

39. New Hampshire's Sculptured Rocks Natural Area features unique rock formations formed by a retreating glacier around 10,000 years ago.

40. New Hampshire features several amusement parks, including Canobie Lake Park and Story Land.

41. The Mount Washington Cog Railway, the world's first of its kind, offers a unique way to ascend the mountain.

42. The Merrimack River is the water source for over 700,000 area residents.

43. Peterborough is home to the first modern public library in the United States.

44. The state bird of New Hampshire is the purple finch. However, the bird is not purple but more of a dark red.

45. As of 2008, the Mount Washington Cog Railway has been powered by biodiesel.

46. The Budweiser Clydesdales were initially trained in New Hampshire up until 2018.

47. The Connecticut River starts in Pittsburg, New Hampshire.

48. New Hampshire's state flower is the purple lilac.

49. The Mt. Washington Auto Road in New Hampshire holds the distinction of being the oldest human-made tourist attraction in the United States, having opened in 1861.

50. The name "chicken tenders" came from the Puritan Backroom, a restaurant in Manchester, New Hampshire. The first usage of the term was in 1974.

NEW JERSEY

1. New Jersey's nickname is the "Garden State" due to its lush landscapes and fertile soil.

2. The world's first boardwalk was built in Atlantic City in 1870.

3. New Jersey is known as the "Diner Capital of the World" for its numerous diners.

4. It has the highest population density of any U.S. state and one of the highest densities of highways and roadways.

5. The first intercollegiate football game was played between Rutgers and Princeton in New Brunswick in 1869.

6. Thomas Edison's laboratory in Menlo Park produced over 400 patents, including the phonograph and the light bulb.

7. Margate City is home to "Lucy the Elephant," a six-story elephant-shaped building.

8. Cape May boasts the largest collection of Victorian homes in the U.S.

9. Atlantic City was the inspiration for the American version of the board game Monopoly.

10. Though located in New York Harbor, the Statue of Liberty is actually closer to New Jersey.

11. Saltwater taffy was first made in Atlantic City.

12. The New Jersey Turnpike is one of the most well-known highways in the U.S.

13. The George Washington Bridge connecting New Jersey and New York is the world's busiest bridge.

14. Hoboken is the birthplace of the legendary singer Frank Sinatra.

15. The hit TV show *The Sopranos* was set in North Caldwell.

16. Island Beach State Park is one of the last remaining barrier islands along the Jersey Shore.

17. At 77 feet (23.5 meters) tall, the Great Falls of the Passaic River in Paterson is one of the nation's largest waterfalls.

18. New Jersey has several indoor water parks for year-round enjoyment.

19. Though part of New York, Ellis Island is in the waters of New Jersey's Jersey City.

20. The first drive-in movie theater in the United States opened in Camden, New Jersey, in 1933.

21. Perth Amboy is one of the oldest cities in the United States, with its earliest European settlement dating back to 1683.

22. Established in 1766, New Jersey is home to Rutgers University, one of the oldest universities in the United States. Rutgers University was originally called Queen's College from 1766 to 1825 before changing names to Rutgers College until 1924. It has been called Rutgers University ever since.

23. New Jersey is known for its unique pork roll, a type of processed meat also called "Taylor ham."

24. New Jersey is the only state where it is illegal to pump your own gas.

25. The first regularly televised bowling show, *Make That Spare*, was broadcast live from the Paramus Bowling Center in Paramus, New Jersey, from 1960 to 1964.

26. New Jersey has a mobile museum. The New Jersey Hall of Fame Museum is on wheels and can be found traveling to schools and events.

27. New Jersey has towns named Cheesequake and Loveladies.

28. Cape May is considered America's "Oldest Seaside Resort," established in the mid-18th century.

29. Bubble wrap was invented in Hawthorne, New Jersey, as a mistake; it was initially intended to be textured wallpaper.

30. North Star Charter School in Newark, New Jersey, has 6,287 students enrolled. The school has 333 teachers.

31. The famous image of George Washington crossing the Delaware River depicts him entering Trenton, New Jersey.

32. There were 296 Revolutionary War battles that took place in New Jersey, the most of many states.

33. At 212 feet (64.6 meters) tall, the Union Watersphere is the second-tallest water sphere in the world, falling six feet (1.8 meters) short of the water spheroid in Edmond, Oklahoma.

34. New Jersey was the first state to ratify the Bill of Rights. It did so on November 20, 1789.

35. Although the first professional baseball game was played in Indiana, the first baseball game actually took place in Hoboken in 1846, 25 years earlier.

36. The famous Hindenburg disaster occurred over Lakehurst, New Jersey.

37. The name New Jersey comes from the English Channel island of Jersey.

38. New Jersey is home to the first Native American Reservation, established in 1758.

39. Atlantic City was home to the very first Miss America Pageant in 1921. Margaret Gorman from Washington, D.C., who was 16 at the time, became the first winner of the pageant.

40. The world's largest working light bulb is in New Jersey. It sits atop a 131-foot (40-meter) tall tower and is 14 feet (1.2 meters) tall.

41. New Jersey was the 3rd state, joining the Union on December 18, 1787.

42. Asbury Park hosts an annual Zombie Walk in October.

43. Paterson used to be known as "Silk City" and had over 120 silk-related businesses dedicated to manufacturing the product.

44. New Jersey is the fourth-smallest state.

45. Princeton and Trenton have both served as the capital of the United States for a brief period of time.

46. George Washington is responsible for choosing New Jersey's colors of buff and dark blue (also known as Jersey blue).

47. New Jersey's capitol building is the third oldest in the country.

48. Only one state in the nation, New Jersey, has all of its counties designated as metropolitan regions.

49. With seven big malls within a 25-mile radius, the state also has the most retail centers in one area.

50. Trenton was named after William Trent and was initially called "Trent's Town."

NEW MEXICO

1. Due to its varied landscapes and rich cultural history, New Mexico is called the "Land of Enchantment."

2. On January 6, 1912, New Mexico became the 47th state in the union.

3. Founded in 1610, Santa Fe is the oldest state capital in the United States.

4. Taos Pueblo is one of the earliest continually inhabited communities in the United States. There is evidence of buildings being built in the area between 1000 and 1450.

5. The 1947 purported UFO event in Roswell made the town renowned.

6. The largest gypsum dune field in the world can be found in White Sands National Park.

7. Beautiful underground caves and formations can be seen at Carlsbad Caverns National Park.

8. As part of the Manhattan Project, Los Alamos, New Mexico, built the first atomic bomb.

9. The world's largest hot air balloon festival is held in Albuquerque, the Albuquerque International Ballon Fiesta.

10. New Mexico is known for its turquoise gemstones.

11. One of North America's longest rivers, the Rio Grande, passes through the state of New Mexico.

12. The Aztec Ruins National Monument is home to ancient Puebloan buildings.

13. Gila Cliff Dwellings National Monument showcases historic cliff ruins created by the Mogollon people.

14. Kasha-Katuwe Tent Rocks National Monument is known for its unusual cone-shaped rock formations.

15. Smokey Bear, the emblem for preventing wildfires, first appeared at The Lincoln National Forest in New Mexico.

16. The Trinity Site, in the White Sands National Park, marks where the first atomic bomb was set off.

17. The annual Zozobra event in Santa Fe includes burning a giant puppet.

18. Green chile peppers are a staple of New Mexican cooking, with the Hatch chile being the most famous.

19. The Chaco Culture National Historical Park is home to stunning architecture and ancient Puebloan ruins.

20. Shiprock is a monadnock standing 1,583 feet (482.5 meters) tall and considered sacred by the Navajo Nation.

21. Valles Caldera is a volcanic crater at the Valles Caldera National Preserve. The crater is 13.7 miles (22 kilometers) wide.

22. Located in Roswell, the New Mexico Military Institute is one of only four junior colleges for the armed forces in the United States. The other three are the Georgia Military College in Milledgeville, Georgia; Marion Military Institute in Marion, Alabama; and Valley Forge Military Academy and College in Wayne, Pennsylvania.

23. The Blue Hole in Santa Rosa is an artesian spring with naturally blue water.

24. The municipality of Roswell proudly hosts events and attractions with an alien theme.

25. Natural hot springs are a draw for a city in New Mexico named Truth or Consequences.

26. The largest state park and reservoir in New Mexico is Elephant Butte Lake.

27. New Mexico State University is home to the Chile Pepper Institute.

28. The Bisti/De-Na-Zin Wilderness area is home to bizarre fossils and rock formations.

29. Ohkay Owingeh Pueblo is one of New Mexico's 19 Pueblos.

30. Originally built in 1610, The San Miguel Mission in Santa Fe, New Mexico, is one of the first churches in the United States and is often called the oldest.

31. The International Space Hall of Fame in Alamogordo recognizes people who have made contributions to space exploration.

32. A battleship named USS New Mexico formerly sailed the seas from 1918 to 1946. It was subsequently scrapped in 1948.

33. Southwestern New Mexico was included in the 1853 Gadsden Purchase, which saw the United States buy land from Mexico by the Treaty of Mesilla.

34. *The Simpsons* TV series is responsible for giving Albuquerque's minor league baseball team its name. The Albuquerque Isotopes played their first game on April 11, 2003.

35. The Ojo Caliente Mineral Springs is one of the only natural health resorts in the world that features Iron, Soda, Arsenic, and Lithia in its sulfur-free water.

36. New Mexico is home to a unique coffee made with the piñon nut.

37. The world's largest pistachio is 30 feet (9 meters) tall and greets visitors to PistachioLand in Alamogordo.

38. There is a town in New Mexico named Pie Town.

39. At 47 feet (14 meters) long, the world's largest chile pepper fittingly calls Las Cruces home.

40. Ordering food in New Mexico is usually followed by the question, "Red or Green?" The question refers to the color of chiles, which is so popular that it is New Mexico's official state question, giving it the distinction of being the only state to have a state question.

41. The Loretto Chapel in Santa Fe features a unique staircase known as the "Miraculous Staircase." The stairs make two complete turns without the support of a central pole.

42. Truth of Consequences is home to the United States' first Spaceport. Spaceport America is home to Virgin Galactic and a few other spaceflight companies.

43. The Tinkertown Museum in Sandia Park features miniature wood-carved scenes and figures.

44. Santa Fe is the highest capital city in the United States. Sitting at 7,199 feet (2,194 meters).

45. Las Vegas, New Mexico, has a population of just over 13,000, making it far smaller than Las Vegas, Nevada.

46. The Rio Grande Gorge Bridge is one of the highest bridges in the United States, standing 650 feet (198 meters) above the river.

47. Albuquerque has more than 300 registered hot air balloon pilots.

48. New Mexico is home to the longest aerial tram in the United States. The Sandia Peak Tramway covers 7,720 feet (2,353 meters), making it the third largest in the world.

49. New Mexico has a natural ice cave that is thousands of years old.

50. The southern region of New Mexico is part of the Chihuahuan Desert.

NEW YORK

1. New York is often called the Empire State, a nickname dating back to the early 19th century.

2. With over 19 million residents, New York is fourth in terms of population in the United States.

3. On July 26, 1788, New York, one of the original 13 colonies, joined the Union as the 11th state.

4. The capital of New York is Albany, one of the country's oldest continually incorporated cities.

5. New York City is made up of five boroughs—Staten Island, Brooklyn, Queens, The Bronx, and Manhattan.

6. New York City's Broadway is renowned for its theaters and is regarded as the height of American theater.

7. From 1892 until 1954, Ellis Island served as the main entry point for immigrants into the United States and processed millions of arrivals.

8. One of the most popular urban parks in the world is the 843-acre (341-hectare) Central Park in Manhattan.

9. France gifted America the Statue of Liberty in 1886, representing liberty and democracy.

10. The first steel-wire suspension bridge in the world was the Brooklyn Bridge, which opened in 1883.

11. New York is home to a portion of Niagara Falls, one of the most well-known natural marvels in the world.

12. The renowned Woodstock Festival, which was significant both musically and culturally, was held in 1969 in Bethel, New York, one and a half hours southwest of Woodstock, New York.

13. The state's economic growth was significantly influenced by the 1825 completion of the Erie Canal.

14. The biggest stock exchange in the world is the New York Stock Exchange (NYSE), which is situated on Wall Street in Manhattan.

15. When the Empire State Building was finished in 1931, it was the highest structure in the entire world. It held the title until 1970.

16. One of the world's most prominent and most renowned art museums is the Metropolitan Museum of Art, or "The Met," which calls New York City home.

17. An international diplomatic center, the United Nations' main office is in New York City.

18. The boardwalk, amusement parks, and renowned hot dog-eating competitions make Coney Island famous.

19. The cultural and artistic movement known as the Harlem Renaissance was centered in Harlem, New York.

20. The largest island in the contiguous United States, Long Island is renowned for its suburban areas and beaches and is the 18th-most populous island in the world.

21. The country's second-largest public library system, the New York Public Library, has almost 53 million items and over 90 locations.

22. The Chrysler Building, which was completed in 1930, is well known for its recognizable Art Deco design.

23. The most linguistically diverse city in the world is New York City, with around 600 different languages spoken.

24. New York borders the Great Lakes and the Atlantic Ocean, the only state to do so.

25. No subway system in the world has more stations than the New York City Subway, which has 472.

26. Central Park has been featured in hundreds of movies and is one of the most recognizable places in America.

27. New York City has the second largest Jewish population of any city. Only Tel Aviv has a higher population. Jerusalem and Haifa, both in Israel, have a smaller Jewish population than New York City.

28. More than 40 buildings in New York City have their own zip code.

29. New York City has over 2,000 pizzerias.

30. The Federal Reserve Building in New York City holds the most significant gold storage reserve in the world.

31. The National Baseball Hall of Fame is in Cooperstown, New York.

32. Eggs Benedict was created in New York City.

33. The historic fort of Fort Ticonderoga participated in both the American Revolutionary War and the French and Indian War.

34. The famous Manhattan complex, Rockefeller Center, is well-known for its ice skating rink, Christmas tree lighting, and other features.

35. Although three National Football League teams bear the New York name, only one actually plays their home games in the state, the Buffalo Bills. The Jets and Giants play their games in New Jersey.

36. The potato chip was invented in Saratoga Springs, New York.

37. The 1820 short story "The Legend of Sleepy Hollow," by Washington Irving, was inspired by the village of Sleepy Hollow.

38. The New York Aquarium in Brooklyn is the country's oldest aquarium still in operation. The aquarium was founded in 1896 and moved to Brooklyn in 1957.

39. One of the biggest Catholic cathedrals in the United States is St. Patrick's Cathedral, a Neo-Gothic structure in Manhattan.

40. In 1837, Tiffany & Co., a well-known jeweler, was established in New York City.

41. The Macy's Thanksgiving Day Parade has been taking place in New York City every year since 1924.

42. One of the biggest urban zoos in the world is the Bronx Zoo.

43. In 1901, Buffalo served as the Pan-American Exposition venue, featuring contemporary technological innovations. President

William McKinley's assassination on the fairgrounds makes the occasion memorable.

44. The Anchor Bar in Buffalo is credited with creating the Buffalo wing in 1964, forever tying the city to this famous dish.

45. A distinctive whispering gallery is situated close to the Oyster Bar & Restaurant in Grand Central Terminal. Because of the acoustics, if you stand in one corner and whisper, someone in the opposite corner can hear you perfectly clear.

46. Under Manhattan's City Hall, there lies a secret, deserted subway stop called "City Hall Station." It was made inaccessible to the general public in 1945, and currently, only specialized excursions are available.

47. Certain New York dogs have been taught to find rats in populated areas to aid in pest control operations.

48. The Empire State Building had a dirigible mast on top when it was finished with the intent of docking airships to it, but it was never used because of security issues.

49. New York City was once named New Amsterdam.

50. New York City is the most populated city in America, with over eight million inhabitants. A number that puts it 30th in the world.

NORTH CAROLINA

1. North Carolina is known for being the place where the Wright brothers conducted the first successful powered airplane flight in Kitty Hawk on December 17, 1903.

2. The "Tar Heel State " nickname is believed to have come from the tar and pitch used to manufacture naval stores.

3. North Carolina joined the Union on November 21, 1789, the 12th state to do so.

4. The Appalachian Mountains in the West and the Outer Banks and coastal regions in the east highlight the state.

5. The Blue Ridge Parkway, often called "America's Favorite Drive," is 469 miles (755 kilometers) long and winds through the scenic Appalachian Mountains in North Carolina.

6. The Research Triangle Park, located near Raleigh, Durham, and Chapel Hill, is a hub for research and innovation, spanning over 7,000 acres (2,833 hectares) and housing numerous technology and biotech companies.

7. Along its coastline, North Carolina is home to various historic lighthouses, including the well-known Cape Hatteras Lighthouse.

8. One of the most heated rivalries in college basketball is that between Duke University and the University of North Carolina at Chapel Hill.

9. The town of Mount Airy served as the model for the made-up community of Mayberry in *The Andy Griffith Show*.

10. With over 175,000 square feet of living area and 250 rooms, the Biltmore Estate near Asheville is the biggest privately owned residence in the country.

11. In the late 1800s, New Bern pharmacist Caleb Bradham invented Pepsi-Cola.

12. Guilford Courthouse National Military Park and other locations pay tribute to North Carolina's pivotal role in the American Revolution.

13. Moonshining has a long history in the Blue Ridge Mountains, and as a result, the customs and culture of the area have been impacted.

14. Blackbeard, a notorious pirate who operated off the coast of North Carolina, was killed in a conflict close to Ocracoke Island.

15. Due to its importance in furniture manufacture and design, High Point is called the "Furniture Capital of the World." It is held twice a year at the High Point Market, which brings in design professionals from all over the world.

16. The state mammal of North Carolina is the Eastern Gray Squirrel.

17. The University of North Carolina at Chapel Hill is the first public university in the United States to hold classes and graduate students, opening its doors in 1795.

18. Beautiful beaches and spectacular sand dunes may be found on the Outer Banks, including the East Coast's tallest natural sand dune system.

19. Winston-Salem has a long history and strong Moravian background.

20. One of the largest military installations in the world by population is in Fayetteville at Fort Bragg, with around 29,000 military personnel.

21. North Carolina has a long history in aviation, including the Wright brothers, and is home to several military and commercial aircraft facilities.

22. Chimney Rock State Park features breathtaking views and a 315-foot (96-meter) tall, recognizable Chimney Rock rock structure.

23. The Carolina Lily is the state's official wildflower.

24. The women of Edenton organized their own tea party in 1774. The Edenton Tea Party was a political demonstration in response to the Tea Act passed by the British Parliament in 1773.

25. The oldest town in North Carolina is Bath, which was settled in the 1690s and has preserved historic buildings.

26. Tobacco, sweet potatoes, and Christmas trees are just a few of the many crops that are produced in large quantities in North Carolina.

27. Wilmington's USS North Carolina Battleship Memorial provides a window into maritime history.

28. Wild horses, thought to be descended from the horses used by Spanish explorers, can be seen on Shackleford Banks and other barrier islands.

29. Despite its name, the New River is one of the world's oldest rivers.

30. The famed Triple Falls may be found in the Dupont State Forest, which is well-known for its waterfalls.

31. The tallest dam in the Eastern United States, Fontana Dam, generates hydroelectricity with a combined capacity of 293.6 megawatts.

32. One of the few swing bridges still in use in North Carolina is the Harkers Island Bridge.

33. Grandfather Mountain was named so because it resembles a human face profile.

34. The Venus flytrap, North Carolina's official state carnivorous plant, grows naturally in North Carolina's coastal plains.

35. At 32 feet (9.75 meters) high, High Point is home to the world's largest chest of drawers.

36. The "Livermush Capital of the World," Shelby, honors this distinctive Southern delicacy prepared with hog liver, head parts, and cornmeal.

37. Babe Ruth's first home run was in Fayetteville, North Carolina.

38. Krispy Kreme originated in Winston-Salem, North Carolina, back in 1937.

39. The White House Christmas Tree has come from North Carolina 14 times, more than any other state.

40. Murphy, North Carolina, is home to the world's largest Ten Commandments. The display can be seen from as high as 5,000 feet (1,524 meters) in the air.

41. North Carolina's state bird is the northern cardinal.

42. The North Carolina Zoo is the largest natural habitat zoo in the world, with 500 acres (202 hectares) of developed land so far.

43. The first gold rush in the United States was in 1799 in Cabarrus County, North Carolina.

44. The NASCAR Hall of Fame is in Charlotte.

45. Winston and Salem were separate cities prior to 1913.

46. North Carolina has the second most breweries per capita at 17 per 50,000 people.

47. North Carolina is home to Mount Mitchell; at 6,684 feet (2,037 meters), it is the highest point east of the Mississippi River.

48. Roanoke Island was home to the first English colony in 1584.

49. The Outer Banks area has been the site of many shipwrecks and is commonly known as the "Graveyard of the Atlantic."

50. North Carolina was the first colony to declare independence from the British.

NORTH DAKOTA

1. North Dakota's nickname is the "Peace Garden State."

2. The capital of North Dakota is Bismarck.

3. Until November 2, 1889, North Dakota was a part of the Dakota Territory.

4. North America's geographic center is Rugby, North Dakota.

5. Over 400 lakes may be found in North Dakota.

6. The Missouri River flows through North Dakota.

7. The vast rural areas and agricultural landscapes of North Dakota are distinctive.

8. The first national parks were created as a result of Theodore Roosevelt's experiences in North Dakota, which influenced his conservation efforts.

9. The state is home to diverse wildlife, including bison, elk, deer, and various bird species.

10. The International Peace Garden, located on the border of Canada and North Dakota, is a symbol of friendship between the two nations.

11. North Dakota was home to a significant number of Minuteman II intercontinental ballistic missile sites during the Cold War.

12. Lake Sakakawea is the second-largest lake in the United States by area.

13. Fargo is the largest city in North Dakota.

14. North Dakota's state flower is the Wild Prairie Rose.

15. Jamestown, North Dakota, is home to the National Buffalo Museum.

16. A bronze statue of Sacagawea, the Shoshone guide of the Lewis and Clark expedition, stands on the grounds of the state capitol in Bismarck.

17. Early settlers of North Dakota were known as "sodbusters" due to the challenges of breaking the tough prairie soil.

18. North Dakota was popular for homesteading in the late 1800s, with the ability to obtain 160 acres of land for free by fulfilling modest requirements established by the Homestead Act.

19. The Missouri and Yellowstone Rivers meet near Williston.

20. There is a city named New England, North Dakota, with a population of less than 1,000.

21. North Dakota has a pyramid that was built in the 1960s to the tune of six billion dollars. The Stanley R. Mickelsen Safeguard

Complex was created as a defense system against the threat of Russian intercontinental ballistic missiles.

22. The Enchanted Highway in North Dakota is dotted with classic and quirky roadside art sculptures.

23. Jamestown has a buffalo statue named Dakota Thunder, standing 26 feet (7.9 meters) tall and weighing 60 tons (54,431 kilograms); it's the largest in the world.

24. Mr. Bubble got its start in North Dakota.

25. Dakota means friend in the Sioux language.

26. The North Dakota State Capitol was finished in 1934 and cost $2 million in total, equivalent to $45.6 million in 2023.

27. North Dakota has less forest land than any other state, with only around 1.5 percent classified as forest land.

28. North Dakota leads the United States in honey production, with over 38 million pounds produced yearly.

29. North Dakota set a world record for the most snow angels made simultaneously in 2007 with 8,962 people.

30. North Dakota is home to the largest grassland in the United States. Little Missouri National Grasslands has an area of more than one million acres (404,685 hectares).

31. Fargo is the only city in the state with more than 100,000 people. It has slightly over 126,000.

32. While only 242 feet (73.76 meters) tall, the North Dakota State Capitol building is the tallest building in the state.

33. North Dakota produces more sunflowers than any other state.

34. North Dakota is home to over 60 Wildlife Refuges, the most in the country.

35. The largest metal sculpture in the world can be found on the Enchanted Highway. The record-setting sculpture stands 110 feet (33.5 meters) tall and is 150 (45.7 meters) feet wide.

36. The Fort Berthold Indian Reservation is 988,000 acres (399,829 hectares), making it roughly the same size as Rhode Island.

37. You can find the town of Buttzville in North Dakota.

38. On multiple occasions, North Dakota has attempted to change its name to simply "Dakota."

39. North Dakota is home to Theodore Roosevelt National Park, the only national park in America named after a single person.

40. North Dakota has around 25 billion tons (22,680 billion kilograms) of brown coal.

41. North Dakota has more churches per capita than any other state.

42. North Dakota and South Dakota became states on the same day, November 2, 1889. The official paperwork was shuffled by President Benjamin Harrison so that neither state could claim they were officially a state before the other.

43. The city of Turtle Lake is home to the "World Champion Turtle Races."

44. North Dakota has the fewest number of national historic landmarks of any state in the United States. The state only has seven total.

45. Protestants outnumber Catholics two to one in the state.

46. Cream of Wheat was born in Grand Forks, North Dakota.

47. It is illegal to dance with a hat on in Fargo.

48. A majority of North Dakota was part of the Louisiana Purchase.

49. English was made the official state language of North Dakota in 1987.

50. North Dakota was once part of New France and New Spain.

OHIO

1. Ohio is often called the "Buckeye State" due to the prevalence of buckeye trees.

2. Ohio was the 17th state to join the United States when it did so on March 1, 1803.

3. Cleveland is home to the Rock and Roll Hall of Fame.

4. Cincinnati can lay claim to having the first professional baseball team. The Cincinnati Red Stockings were formed in 1869.

5. The first hospital-based ambulance service in the United States began in 1865 in Cincinnati, Ohio.

6. Eight presidents of the United States were born in Ohio.

7. The state bird is the northern cardinal.

8. Cincinnati is home to the first established professional and fully paid fire department in the United States, which came to be on April 1, 1853.

9. The Cleveland Clinic is one of the world's largest and most renowned medical centers.

10. Sandusky's Cedar Point amusement park is known as the "Roller Coaster Capital of the World." It currently has 16 roller coasters.

11. Canton, Ohio, is the home of the Pro Football Hall of Fame.

12. Astronaut Neil Armstrong, the first person to walk on the moon, was born in Wapakoneta, Ohio, and died in Cincinnati, Ohio.

13. Ohio has many islands in Lake Erie, including Kelleys Island and Put-in-Bay.

14. In 1914, Cleveland installed the world's first electric traffic signal.

15. The Goodyear Tire and Rubber Company was founded in 1898 in Akron, Ohio.

16. Ohio's state reptile is the black racer snake.

17. Bellefontaine, Ohio, is home to the oldest concrete street in the United States. It was installed in 1891.

18. Oberlin College in Oberlin, Ohio, was one of the first colleges to admit African Americans.

19. Columbus, Ohio, the capital of Ohio, has a German village.

20. Ohio has its own treat called a buckeye. The treat is made with peanut butter fudge and chocolate to resemble the nut of the buckeye tree.

21. The movie *The Shawshank Redemption* was filmed at the Ohio State Reformatory.

22. Sugarcreek, Ohio, is home to the world's largest cuckoo clock at 23 feet (7 meters) tall.

23. Dublin, Ohio, has a unique art installation of giant concrete ears of corn planted in the ground known as Cornhenge.

24. Ohio's state beverage is Tomato Juice.

25. Laceyville, Ohio, a former town, was permanently submerged with the creation of Tappan Lake.

26. The Wright Brothers' first plane was designed and built in Dayton, Ohio.

27. The Buckeye tree is the official state tree of Ohio.

28. The Ohio State University is the 3rd largest university by enrollment in the United States.

29. The Akron Police Department was the first to use a police car. The electric wagon could reach speeds of up to 16 miles per hour (26 kilometers per hour) and was first used in 1899.

30. Cedar Point is the second oldest amusement park still in operation, having opened in 1870.

31. The National Museum of the United States Air Force is in Dayton, Ohio.

32. Superman was created in Cleveland by Jerry Siegel and Joe Shuster. The character was sold to Detective Comics, Inc. for $130.

33. Ohio has an Amish population of over 80,000 members, the 2nd highest in the United States.

34. Ohio is the only state whose state flag is not rectangular.

35. The Beer Barrel in Put-in-Bay has the longest bar in the world. The bar measures 405 feet (123 meters) long and has 160 bar stools.

36. There is only 1,094 feet (333 meters) of difference between Ohio's highest and lowest elevations.

37. During the Civil War, more Union soldiers came from Ohio than from any other state.

38. Ohio is known as the "Birthplace of Aviation."

39. Marietta, named after Queen Marie Antoinette of France, was the first permanent settlement in Ohio.

40. Roughly 80 percent of Ohio's population lives in urban areas.

41. Chillicothe and Zanesville were originally the capitals of Ohio.

42. Four of the eight presidents from Ohio (William Henry Harrison was elected while a resident of Ohio but was born in Virginia) have died while in office.

43. The world's largest basket is seven stories high and more than 200 feet (61 meters) wide. It can be found in Newark, Ohio.

44. Both Arby's and Wendy's were founded in Ohio.

45. Warren, Ohio, is home to the largest drumsticks in the world. The sticks can be found at the entrance of Dave Grohl Alley. The alley is named after Dave Grohl, a famous musician who is currently a member of the Foo Fighters and who previously was the drummer for Nirvana and Queens of the Stone Age. Dave Grohl was born in Warren, Ohio, in 1969.

46. Ohio was officially admitted to the union in 1953, 150 years after it filed the necessary paperwork to be declared a state. The state is given a retroactive date of admission to the union of 1803.

47. The word Ohio originates from the Iroquois word meaning "great river."

48. Ohio has hundreds of old burial mounds throughout the state.

49. Around 50 percent of the population of the United States lives within 500 miles (805 kilometers) of Columbus, Ohio.

50. Cincinnati is home to a chain of restaurants named Skyline Chili, known for Cincinnati chili. A dish of spaghetti topped with chili and shredded cheese, although some prefer it with onions and beans as well.

OKLAHOMA

1. Oklahoma became the 46th state of the United States on November 16, 1907.

2. Oklahoma is often called the "Sooner State," named after settlers who arrived sooner than they were expected to arrive.

3. The state capital is Oklahoma City.

4. One of the largest collections of Art Deco buildings in the United States is found in Tulsa.

5. One of the major Air Force maintenance and repair facilities is located at Tinker AFB in Oklahoma City.

6. The largest tallgrass prairie preserve in the world is the Williams Tallgrass Prairie Preserve in Osage County, Oklahoma.

7. Oklahoma's panhandle is a remote area with a distinctive landscape.

8. The Golden Driller statue in Tulsa is the sixth largest statue in the United States, standing 75 feet (23 meters) tall and weighing 43,500 pounds (19,700 kilograms).

9. The First Americans Museum in Oklahoma City celebrates the state's Native American heritage.

10. The National Softball Hall of Fame resides in Oklahoma City's Adventure District.

11. Lake Eufaula, a reservoir, is the largest-capacity lake in Oklahoma.

12. Oklahoma City's airport is named after Will Rogers. Will Rogers was a famous Native American vaudeville performer.

13. The only city in the contiguous United States to be bombed during World War II was Boise City, Oklahoma. The U.S. Army accidentally dropped the bombs during a training mission. There were no casualties due to the bombing.

14. Sonic Drive-In was founded in 1953 in Shawnee, Oklahoma.

15. Cimarron County, located in the panhandle, is the only county in the United States that touches four other states: Kansas, Texas, New Mexico, and Colorado.

16. Oklahoma City is Oklahoma's second capital, the original being Guthrie.

17. The National Wrestling Hall of Fame in Stillwater, Oklahoma, celebrates amateur wrestling of the freestyle and Greco-Roman variety.

18. Oklahoma has a town named Gene Autry, which was named after the actor himself.

19. Oklahoma's state wildflower is the Indian blanket.

20. The Red River forms most of Oklahoma's southern border with Texas.

21. Although Oklahoma is landlocked, there is a blue whale on Route 66 just outside Catoosa, Oklahoma, named the Blue Whale of Catoosa.

22. Oklahoma City has a museum dedicated to the study of bones, the Oklahoma City Museum of Osteology.

23. Oklahoma's state fruit is the strawberry.

24. Oklahoma has an official state meal consisting of fried okra, cornbread, barbecue pork, squash, biscuits, sausage and gravy, grits, corn, strawberries, chicken fried steak, pecan pie, and black-eyed peas.

25. Inola, Oklahoma, is known as the "Hay Capital of the World" due to its high-quality hay grown there.

26. Beaver, Oklahoma, hosts the World Cow Chip Throwing Contest, where contestants see who can throw dried cow dung the furthest.

27. The world's first parking meter was installed in Oklahoma City.

28. The Red River gives name to the football game between Oklahoma and Texas, commonly known as the "Red River Showdown" or "Red River Rivalry."

29. Edmond, Oklahoma, is home to the world's tallest water sphere. The water spheroid is 218 feet (66 meters) tall.

30. The American Banjo Museum and Hall of Fame is in Oklahoma City.

31. Parts of four distinct mountain ranges can be found in Oklahoma: the Ouachitas, Arbuckles, Wichitas, and the Ozarks.

32. Oklahoma has more than 200 manmade lakes, the most in the United States.

33. A mountain smaller than 2,000 feet (610 meters) high is considered a hill, and as such, Cavanal Hill near Poteau, Oklahoma, is the "World's Highest Hill," with an elevation of 1,999 feet (609 meters).

34. The Ed Galloway Totem Pole Park on Route 66 in Oklahoma is the "World's Tallest Concrete Totem Pole" at 60 feet (18 meters) tall.

35. The only Iodine produced in the United States comes from Oklahoma.

36. Due to the weathering of sands, siltstone, and shale, red dirt can be found on more than one million acres (404,686 hectares) in Oklahoma.

37. Girl Scout Cookies were sold for the first time in 1917 in Muskogee, Oklahoma.

38. Oklahoma has the second-highest Native American population by percentage behind Alaska.

39. Oklahoma's name comes from the Choctaw language, meaning red people. "Okla" means people, and "humma" means red.

40. Oklahoma is one of three states in the United States that produce helium. The other two are Kansas and Texas.

41. Oklahoma's state vegetable is Watermelon, a fruit.

42. In 2009, the city of Picher was declared too toxic to be habitable, leading to a max exodus of the city. In 2013, Picher was officially dissolved.

43. The American Pigeon Museum can be found in Oklahoma City.

44. The Cherokee Nation is headquartered in Tahlequah, Oklahoma.

45. Two-thirds of Oklahoma's population reside in either the Oklahoma City or Tulsa metropolitan areas.

46. The Oklahoma State Capitol building has an oil well beneath it, the only capital in the world with that distinction.

47. The American Airlines maintenance base in Tulsa spans 33 acres (13 hectares), making it the world's largest airline maintenance facility.

48. Oklahoma is the largest producer of gypsum in the United States.

49. Shopping Carts were invented in Oklahoma and first appeared at the Humpty Dumpty supermarket chain, having been created by its owner.

50. Oklahoma still allows death by firing squad in case lethal injection, nitrogen hypoxia, or electrocution are not available or are found to be unconstitutional.

OREGON

1. Oregon became the 33rd state of the United States on February 14, 1859.

2. Oregon is often called the "Beaver State."

3. The state capital of Oregon is Salem.

4. Oregon is home to Crater Lake, which is the deepest lake in the United States at 1,949 feet (594 meters) deep.

5. Mount Hood is the highest mountain in Oregon. A dormant stratovolcano, Mount Hood measures 11,249 feet (3,429 meters) in height.

6. The Columbia River Gorge is known for its stunning waterfalls and breathtaking scenery.

7. Portland is the largest city in Oregon.

8. In 1805, Lewis and Clark's expedition reached the Oregon coast.

9. Oregon is home to Hells Canyon, a ten-mile-wide canyon creating the deepest river gorge in North America at 7,993 feet (2,436 meters).

10. Powell's City of Books in Portland, Oregon, is the world's largest independent bookstore and home to over one million books.

11. Multnomah Falls is a 620-foot (189-meter) tall waterfall and a popular tourist destination. It is the tallest waterfall in Oregon.

12. Cannon Beach is famous for its iconic Haystack Rock and stunning coastline.

13. There are 61 volcanoes in Oregon.

14. Sea Lion Caves on the Oregon Coast is America's largest sea cave.

15. Astoria, Oregon, founded in 1811, was the first permanent settlement in the United States west of the Rocky Mountains.

16. Oregon sunstone is the state's official gemstone.

17. The Willamette Valley is a major agricultural region known for its wine production, with over 500 wineries. It is most famous for its Pinot Noir varietal.

18. The Portland Japanese Garden inside Washington Park is widely considered one of the most authentic Japanese gardens outside of Japan.

19. The Oregon Symphony was founded in 1896, making it the sixth-oldest orchestra in the United States.

20. Oregon's Beach Bill was passed in 1967 to preserve public access to all of Oregon's beaches.

21. Forest Park in Portland, at 7,172 acres (2,902 hectares), is one of the largest urban forest reserves in the United States.

22. The Oregon spotted frog, Oregon white oak, and Oregon silverspot butterfly are just a few of the unusual creatures unique to Oregon.

23. Oregon is home to the Painted Hills, part of the John Day Fossil Beds National Monument, which is a colorful geological formation in Wheeler County.

24. The Oregon Shakespeare Festival in Ashland, Oregon, is one of the largest Shakespearean festivals in the United States.

25. Nike, known globally for its footwear, was founded in Eugene, Oregon, by Phil Knight and Bill Bowerman in 1964. It maintains its headquarters in Beaverton, Oregon.

26. Washington Park is home to the International Rose Test Garden and is home to over 10,000 rose bushes and around 650 different varieties.

27. At over 72 feet (22 meters) tall, the world's largest barber pole can be found in Forest Grove, Oregon.

28. Portland, Oregon, has many nicknames, including "The City of Roses" or "Rose City," "Stumptown," "Rip City," "PDX," and "Bridgetown."

29. The world's largest living organism can be found in Oregon's Malheur National Forest. The giant *Armillaria ostoyae*, a fungus, is estimated to be over 2,400 years old and spans over 2,385 acres (965 hectares).

30. Portland is home to Mill Ends Park, the world's smallest park. The park is a mere two feet (.6 meters) across and has an area of 452 square inches (.29 square meters). The park is home to a single tree and is located on a median strip.

31. Goat Yoga began in Albany, Oregon.

32. The D River in Lincoln City was once the shortest river in the world at 440 feet (134 meters). The D River lost its title in 1989 to Montana's Roe River.

33. Portland is home to the Shanghai Tunnels, a series of underground passageways mainly under the Old Town Chinatown neighborhood.

34. The Rogue River-Siskiyou National Forest has a permanently installed Bigfoot trap.

35. Although it was started in Zaragoza, Spain, Portland's World Naked Bike Ride is the world's largest, with over 10,000 riders.

36. The movie *Free Willy* was primarily filmed in Oregon.

37. Oregon is home to the third largest Alpaca population in the United States.

38. Portland, Oregon, was named after Portland, Maine.

39. The one-way street originated in Eugene, Oregon.

40. Oregon is the only state in the United States with a state flag that features different images on the obverse and reverse sides.

41. Oregon's official state nut is the hazelnut.

42. Oregon has eight distinct major regions: Central Oregon, Eastern Oregon, Mount Hood, the Oregon Coast, Portland, Southern Oregon, the Willamette Valley, and the Columbia Gorge.

43. More than 60 Native American tribes have called Oregon home.

44. In Oregon's history, it has been claimed by Great Britain, Russia, Spain, France, and now the United States.

45. The Columbia River Gorge has over 90 waterfalls.

46. The Oregon Trail started in Missouri and ended in Oregon City, Oregon.

47. The town of Springfield in "The Simpsons" was named after Springfield, Oregon.

48. Oregon initially prohibited the consumption of alcoholic beverages in 1844. This original prohibition was repealed in 1845.

49. A coin flip selected Portland's name. The other potential name was Boston.

50. The 1994 Oregon Death with Dignity Act made Oregon the first state to legalize physician-assisted dying.

PENNSYLVANIA

1. Pennsylvania became the second state of the United States on December 12, 1787.

2. Pennsylvania is often called the "Keystone State."

3. The state capital is Harrisburg.

4. The Liberty Bell in Philadelphia is an iconic symbol of American independence.

5. The Declaration of Independence was adopted in Philadelphia on July 4, 1776.

6. The Constitutional Convention of 1787 was held in Philadelphia to draft the U.S. Constitution.

7. Opening in 1751, Pennsylvania Hospital in Philadelphia was one of the first hospitals in the United States.

8. The Philadelphia Zoo was the first public zoo in the United States.

9. Pittsburgh, Pennsylvania, has 446 bridges, more than any other city in America.

10. Philadelphia served as the capital of the United States from 1790 to 1800.

11. Pittsburgh was known as the "Steel City" due to its prominence in the steel industry.

12. Pennsylvania is home to the largest Amish population in the world, with most residing in Lancaster County.

13. Punxsutawney Phil, the famous groundhog who predicts the weather on Groundhog Day, hails from Punxsutawney, Pennsylvania.

14. Hershey, Pennsylvania, is home to the Hershey chocolate company.

15. Gettysburg, Pennsylvania, is home to one of the most famous and significant battles of the Civil War, known as the Battle of Gettysburg.

16. Eastern State Penitentiary is located in Pennsylvania. This former prison in Philadelphia is famous for its architecture and history of notable inmates, including Al Capone and Willie Sutton.

17. The Monongahela and Allegheny Rivers meet in downtown Pittsburgh to form the Ohio River.

18. The University of Pennsylvania School of Medicine was the first medical school in the United States.

19. Lancaster is home to Lancaster Central Market, the oldest farmers' market in the country, dating back to 1730.

20. Pennsylvania Dutch refers to the German-speaking Amish and Mennonite communities.

21. Valley Forge National Historical Park in King of Prussia, Pennsylvania, commemorates the site of the Continental Army's winter encampment.

22. The Betsy Ross House in Philadelphia is the legendary birthplace of the American flag.

23. Fallingwater, one of the most famous designs of Frank Lloyd Wright, is in Mill Run, Pennsylvania.

24. A statue of the fictional character Rocky Balboa stands near the Philadelphia Museum of Art.

25. Latrobe, Pennsylvania, is home to the first Banana Split. It was created by David "Doc" Stickler, an optometrist, in 1904.

26. Kinzua Bridge in Kinzua Bridge State Park was built in 1882 and, at the time, was the highest railway bridge in the world, standing 301 feet (92 meters) above the terrain below. The majority of the bridge was destroyed by a tornado in 2003.

27. Pennsylvania's official state dog breed is the Great Dane.

28. The Tomb of the Unknown Revolutionary War Soldier in Philadelphia's Washington Square is the first monument in the United States to an unknown soldier.

29. The Andy Warhol Museum in Pittsburgh celebrates the life and art of the pop artist.

30. The Costco in Lancaster, Pennsylvania, has a dedicated area to park a horse and buggy in response to the large Amish population of the area.

31. The Rockville Stone Arch Bridge is the longest stone masonry arch railroad bridge ever built. It travels a distance of 3,820 feet (1164 meters).

32. Independence Hall in Philadelphia is where both the Declaration of Independence and the Constitution were debated and adopted.

33. The mountain laurel is Pennsylvania's official state flower.

34. Pennsylvania borders Lake Erie and six states: New York, New Jersey, Delaware, Maryland, West Virginia, and Ohio.

35. Pennsylvania was named after the well-known William Penn's father, who was also named Wiliam Penn. The name is Latin, meaning "Penn's woods."

36. The first computer, the Electronic Numerical Integrator and Computer (ENIAC), was invented at the University of Pennsylvania, being completed in 1945. The project cost $487,000.00 at the time. The price would equate to $8.1 million in 2023.

37. In 1783, The Pennsylvania Evening Post became the first daily newspaper published in America.

38. Pennsylvania is the only one of the original 13 colonies that does not border the Atlantic Ocean.

39. During World War II, the Philadelphia Eagles and Pittsburgh Steelers football teams merged to form the Philadelphia-Pittsburgh "Steagles." Both teams were short players due to those who left to fight the war.

40. The land of Pennsylvania was a gift to William Penn from King Charles I.

41. Philadelphia's City Hall has more than five times as many rooms as the White House. With 700 rooms, it is the largest municipal building in the United States.

42. Bubble gum was invented by an accountant in Philadelphia back in 1928.

43. The Big Mac was first sold to the public at a McDonald's in Uniontown, Pennsylvania.

44. Kennett Square, Pennsylvania, is the leading producer of Mushrooms in the United States. The area produces almost 50 percent of the United States' mushrooms.

45. Yuengling, the oldest operating brewing company in America, started in Pottsville, Pennsylvania, and is still headquartered in the city.

46. Eastern State Penitentiary had central heating before the advancement could be found in the White House.

47. Jonas Salk is responsible for the first effective polio vaccine. He developed with a team at the University of Pittsburgh.

48. Leap the Dips is the name of the oldest operating roller coaster in the world. It is located at Lakemont Park in Altoona, Pennsylvania, and opened in 1902.

49. Moravian Book Shop, located in Bethlehem, Pennsylvania, is the 2nd oldest continuously operating bookstore in the world, having opened in 1745.

50. The original Ferris Wheel was built in Pittsburgh, Pennsylvania, by Ferris & Co. and debuted at the 1893 World's Columbian Exposition in Chicago, Illinois.

RHODE ISLAND

1. Rhode Island is known as the "Ocean State" due to its extensive coastline.

2. Rhode Island is the smallest state in the United States by land area.

3. Rhode Island was the 13th state to join the Union on May 29, 1790.

4. The state capital is Providence.

5. The Newport Mansions, known for their Gilded Age architecture, are a popular tourist attraction.

6. Roger Williams founded the colony of Rhode Island in 1636 when he fled religious persecution in Massachusetts.

7. In 1774, Rhode Island was the first colony to call for a Continental Congress.

8. Rhode Island became the first colony to declare independence from Britain. It did so on May 4, 1776.

9. The state bird is the Rhode Island Red chicken.

10. Brown University, founded in 1764, is one of the oldest Ivy League institutions. It was initially known as the College in the English Colony of Rhode Island and Providence Plantations. It changed its name to Brown University in 1804 in honor of Nicholas Brown, a businessman and prominent benefactor of the school.

11. The Breakers in Newport, a summer residence for Cornelius Vanderbilt II, is one of the most famous Newport Mansions.

12. The Newport Folk Festival started in 1959 and is one of the oldest music festivals in the U.S.

13. Rhode Island is only 37 miles (60 kilometers) wide and 48 miles (77 kilometers) long.

14. The state motto is "Hope."

15. The U.S. Industrial Revolution began in 1793 at Samuel Slater's Slater Mill in Pawtucket, Rhode Island.

16. The International Tennis Hall of Fame is in Newport, Rhode Island.

17. The dome on the Rhode Island State House has a self-supported marble dome. It is the fourth largest marble dome in the world that is self-supported.

18. The world's largest artificial bug, Nibbles Woodaway (also known as the "Big Blue Bug"), is in Providence, Rhode Island.

19. Rhode Island is home to the oldest lending library in the United States, the Redwood Library and Athenaeum, which is in Newport.

20. The first Baptist congregation in North America was established by Roger Williams in Providence.

21. Quahog is the official state shell of Rhode Island.

22. In 1652, Rhode Island passed a law freeing an enslaved after ten years of service, the first law against slavery in the Country.

23. The tallest point in Rhode Island, Jerimoth Hill, is only 812 feet (247 meters) above sea level.

24. The Industrial National Bank Building, also known as the "Superman Building," was the tallest building in New England outside of Boston when it was built in 1928. At 428 feet (130 meters), it is now the 28th tallest building in New England.

25. There are more than 30 islands in Narragansett Bay.

26. The Crawford Street Bridge in downtown Providence was once the world's widest bridge at 1,147 feet (340 meters) wide.

27. The Fourth of July Parade in Bristol, Rhode Island, is the oldest continuous Independence Day celebration in the United States, being founded in 1785.

28. The Point Judith Light is a lighthouse in Narragansett Bay that has been standing since 1856. It was initially completed in 1810 but was destroyed by a hurricane in 1815, replaced in 1816, and eventually replaced with the current structure in 1856.

29. Rhode Island's state motto, "Hope," is the shortest of any U.S. state.

30. WaterFire, a sculpture by Barnaby Evans, has been illuminating the Woonasquatucket River with fire since 1994.

31. The official state drink of Rhode Island is coffee milk, a sweet coffee-flavored milk beverage.

32. Until 2020, the official name of Rhode Island was "State of Rhode Island and Providence Plantations."

33. Benefit Street in Providence is known as the "Mile of History" due to its historic architecture.

34. The Superman Building in Providence gets its nickname from resembling the Daily Planet building in Superman comics.

35. The Newport Tower is a mysterious stone tower with an uncertain origin. It has a height of 28 feet (8.5 meters). It is also known as "Touro Tower," "Viking Tower," "Round Tower," and "Newport Stone Tower."

36. The oldest and most northern topiary garden in the United States is in Portsmouth, Rhode Island. The Green Animals Topiary Garden covers seven acres (2.8 hectares) and has more than 80 sculpted plants.

37. The Slater Mill was the first water-powered cotton spinning mill in the United States.

38. Newport, Rhode Island, was home to the first U.S. Open golf tournament. The event in 1895 had 11 golfers, and the grand prize was $150.

39. Despite being the smallest state in the United States, Rhode Island has 400 miles (643.7 kilometers) of coastline.

40. The town of Woonsocket hosts the annual "Autumnfest," one of the largest autumn celebrations in New England.

41. The Westchester Polo Club in Newport was the first polo club in the United States. The club was formed in 1876.

42. The White Horse Tavern in Newport, Rhode Island, is the oldest restaurant in the United States, having been open since 1673.

43. Newport is home to the Touro Synagogue, founded in 1658; it is the oldest synagogue in North America.

44. The Rhode Island capital building has a statue on the top called "The Independent Man."

45. Idawalley Zoradia Lewis is the only person to have a lighthouse named after them. The former lighthouse keeper maintained the Lime Rock Light, whose name was later changed to the Ida Lewis Rock Lighthouse.

46. Rhode Island is home to Cumberlandite, a type of igneous rock. Rhode Island is the only place where the rock is found.

47. Rhode Island has the most shipwrecks per square mile of anyway.

48. Rhode Island never ratified the Eighteenth Amendment. However, it complied with the laws of prohibition.

49. Although Rhode Island is the smallest state, it has 13 accredited, degree-granting institutions spread throughout.

50. The first section of road in the United States to be lit by street lights was Pelham Street in Newport in 1803, thanks to the invention of gas lights by William Murdoch.

SOUTH CAROLINA

1. South Carolina's official nickname is the "Palmetto State."

2. South Carolina was the eighth state to ratify the U.S. Constitution, doing so in 1788.

3. The capital of South Carolina is Columbia.

4. Charleston is the largest city in South Carolina.

5. The state dance is the shag, a style of swing dance.

6. Fort Sumter, in Charleston Harbor, was the site of the first shots fired in the Civil War. Confederate troops fired on the fort at 4:30 A.M. on April 12, 1861.

7. The state motto is "Dum spiro spero," which means "While I breathe, I hope."

8. The Charleston Tea Garden is the only large-scale tea plantation in the U.S.

9. The Carolina Reaper, one of the world's hottest chili peppers, was bred in Rock Hill, South Carolina.

10. The official state flower is the yellow jessamine.

11. Congaree National Park is almost 27,000 acres (10,927 hectares) and includes the largest intact expanse of old-growth bottomland hardwood forest remaining in the southeastern United States.

12. The Great Pee Dee River originates in the Appalachian Mountains.

13. South Carolina is known for its whole-hog BBQ.

14. The Palmetto Trail is currently a 350-mile-long (563-kilometer) trail through South Carolina created for recreational hiking and biking.

15. South Carolina is home to eight military bases that include every branch of the armed forces, with the exception of the Coast Guard.

16. South Carolina is home to the Gullah-Geechee Cultural Heritage Corridor, a federal National Heritage Area that represents the significant history of the Gullah-Geechee people and maintains their cultural traditions.

17. The City Market in downtown Charleston is a historic four-city block market established in the 1790s.

18. The Port of Charleston is the 4th busiest container port on the east coast.

19. The South Carolina Botanical Garden features one of the largest collections of nature-based sculptures in the United States. The Garden is located on the campus of Clemson University in Clemson, South Carolina.

20. Irmo, South Carolina, hosts the Irmo Okra Strut, a festival that celebrates okra.

21. Angel Oak Park on Johns Island is home to a Southern live oak that is between 400 and 500 years old.

22. South Carolina's official state vegetable is collard greens.

23. South Carolina has two state songs. "Carolina" and "South Carolina On My Mind" are both recognized.

24. South Carolina is second only to California in how many peaches it grows.

25. Charleston is named after King Charles II and was originally named Charles Town.

26. Before 1712, South Carolina and North Carolina were jointly known as the Province of Carolina.

27. Morgan Island is home to a colony of free-ranging rhesus monkeys and has been given the nickname of "Monkey Island." The island is home to over 3,500 monkeys.

28. South Carolina previously had another nickname, the "Iodine State." Due to the high levels of iodine found in the vegetation, the state briefly adopted the nickname from 1930 to 1935, and even included the word "Iodine" on the state's license plates.

29. South Carolina was the site of more than 200 Revolutionary War battles.

30. English settlers were the first to build a settlement in what is known today as South Carolina. The French and Spanish had discovered the region earlier but never settled the area.

31. South Carolina seceded from the United States on December 20, 1860, in response to the election of Abraham Lincoln as United States president. It was the first state to do so.

32. The largest Ginkgo biloba farm in the world is in Sumter, South Carolina.

33. The South Carolina Department of Education is the only state whose school department owns and maintains its school bus fleet.

34. The College of Charleston was founded in 1770. It is the oldest higher education institution south of Virginia and the 13th oldest in the U.S.

35. Summerville, South Carolina, is "The Birthplace of Sweet Tea."

36. The Charleston Museum in downtown Charleston was America's First Museum when it opened in 1773.

37. Brookgreen Gardens is home to over 1,440 American figurative sculptures, one of the world's largest collections of outdoor sculptures.

38. The official state snack of South Carolina is boiled peanuts.

39. Myrtle Beach is the 4th most visited beach in America in terms of annual visitors. The beach brings in over 10 million visitors a year.

40. The Town Theatre in Columbia was built in 1924 and is one of the first community theaters in the United States.

41. Although a German company, BMW manufactures most of its SUV models in Spartanburg, South Carolina.

42. South Carolina has the lowest percentage of women in the state legislature of any state. Less than 11 percent of legislators in the state are women.

43. The Topper archaeological site in South Carolina is an important site in determining the earliest human habitation in North America.

44. At one point in the 1730s, more than two-thirds of the population of South Carolina was of African descent.

45. Charleston was the first capital of South Carolina.

46. South Carolina rejoined the Union in 1868—eight years after it had decided to secede.

47. South Carolina was home to at least 29 distinct groups of Native Americans.

48. Charleston's Rivers High School became the first racially integrated high school in South Carolina in 1963.

49. The largest agricultural crop in South Carolina, based on value, is timber.

50. Myrtle Beach's population is just over 35,000, yet it is home to more than 85 golf courses.

SOUTH DAKOTA

1. South Dakota's official nickname is the "Mount Rushmore State."

2. The capital of South Dakota is Pierre.

3. South Dakota is technically considered part of the Midwestern region of the United States.

4. South Dakota is home to Mount Rushmore National Memorial, which features the heads of four previous presidents sculpted into the face of the Black Hills. The four faces are George Washington, Thomas Jefferson, Theodore Roosevelt, and Abraham Lincoln.

5. South Dakota is known for its vast prairies, rolling hills, and expansive farmland.

6. The official state bird is the ring-necked pheasant.

7. The Black Hills is a sacred site for many Native Americans.

8. Sturgis, South Dakota, is home to the Sturgis Motorcycle Rally, which draws in 500,000 - 700,000+ attendees annually over a ten-day span.

9. The Corn Palace in Mitchell, South Dakota, is a Moorish Revival building with murals and designs covering the building made from corn and other grains, unveiling a new design each year.

10. Wind Cave National Park was the sixth national park in the United States and the first cave to be designated as a national park in the world.

11. Kuchen, a German pastry, officially became the state dessert of South Dakota on July 1, 2000.

12. Custer State Park is home to the Buffalo Roundup, where annually, on the last Thursday of September, around 1,300 bison are herded. The event is so popular that it is now available to watch via a live stream feed.

13. South Dakota is known for its rich Native American heritage.

14. The Crazy Horse Memorial is a sculpture being carved out of Thunderhead Mountain in Crazy Horse, South Dakota. The sculpture has been in progress since 1948.

15. Rapid City is home to the "The City of Presidents," which features life-sized statues of former presidents of the United States.

16. South Dakota has a rich cowboy and ranching history.

17. De Smet, South Dakota, embraces its ties to Laura Ingalls Wilder, author of "Little House on the Prairie."

18. The Black Hills region is home to diverse wildlife, including bison and elk.

19. The state's official fossil is the triceratops.

20. The Harney Peak Fire Tower atop Black Elk Peak sits at 7,242 feet (2,207 meters), making it the highest structure east of the Rocky Mountains.

21. At 50 feet (15.24 meters) tall, the sculpture "Dignity of Earth and Sky" near Chamberlain, South Dakota, is one of the largest statues in the United States. The sculpture honors the culture of the Dakota and Lakota people.

22. The Homestake Mine in Lead, South Dakota, was North America's largest and deepest gold mine. Prior to closing in 2002, the mine was 8,000 feet (2,438 meters) deep.

23. The Needles Highway is a 14-mile (22.5-kilometer) road that features narrow tunnels, stunning rock formations, and winding roads requiring extra caution.

24. Rapid City, South Dakota, is home to Chapel in the Hills, a stave church that is an exact replica of the Borgund stave church in Norway.

25. The Wall Drug Store in Wall is a famous roadside attraction made up of a collection of cowboy-themed stores offering various goods and free ice water and displaying over 300 original oil paintings.

26. The Pioneer Auto Museum in Murdo, South Dakota, has more than 275 classic cars on display.

27. If the Crazy Horse Memorial sculpture is completed as designed, it would stand 641 feet (195 meters) long and 563 feet (172 meters) tall, making it the second tallest statue in the world as of 2023.

28. The Black Hills is home to Hippie Hole, a popular swimming spot with a small waterfall.

29. Calamity Jane and Wild Bill Hickock are both buried in Deadwood, South Dakota.

30. Storybook Island is a free children's theme park with storybook characters in Rapid City.

31. The Geographic Center of the Nation Monument can be found in Belle Fourche, South Dakota. However, the monument is not actually placed at the geographic center of the United States due to the actual location being on private land.

32. Hot Springs, South Dakota, is home to an active paleontological dig site where mammoth fossils have been discovered. The Mammoth Site also has a museum.

33. South Dakota is home to Badlands National Park, which spans 244,000 acres (98,743 hectares).

34. The Homestake Mine was home to an underground laboratory in the mid-1960s, which was the first to observe solar neutrinos, a neutral fermion originating from nuclear fusion in the Sun's core.

35. South Dakota was once part of The Dakota Territory, which included North Dakota and parts of present-day Wyoming, Montana, and Nebraska.

36. South Dakota is home to nine Native American tribes: the Cheyenne River Sioux Tribe, the Sisseton Wahpeton Oyate, the Crow Creek Sioux Tribe, the Flandreau Santee Sioux Tribe, the Rosebud Sioux Tribe, the Lower Brule Sioux Tribe, the Oglala Sioux Tribe, the Standing Rock Sioux Tribe, and the Yankton Sioux Tribe.

37. South Dakota's capital, Pierre, is only larger than Montpelier, Vermont, in terms of population, making it the second smallest capital city in the United States.

38. South Dakota's previous nicknames have included the "Sunshine State," "Coyote State," and "Blizzard State."

39. South Dakota has four cows on average for every person, making it the highest ratio of cows to people in the United States.

40. The Mount Rushmore sculpture took 14 years to complete.

41. The Minuteman Missile National Historic Site in Philip, South Dakota, is the last publicly-known intact Minuteman II intercontinental ballistic missile launching system in the United States.

42. South Dakota leads the United States when it comes to Bison meat production.

43. Badlands National Park is home to 206 species of birds.

44. It is illegal to fall asleep in a cheese factory in South Dakota.

45. Ben Reifel, whose Lakota Sioux name was Lone Feather, was the first Sioux Native American to be elected and serve in the House of Representatives. Lone Feather served five terms.

46. The Fischer quintuplets, born to Mary Ann Fischer, were the first known surviving set of quintuplets born in America. They were born on September 14, 1963, in Aberdeen, South Dakota.

47. Mount Rushmore is named after an attorney from New York, Charles E. Rushmore. Mr. Rushmore made a $5,000.00 donation towards the sculpture in 1925, and in 1930, the name was officially recognized as Mount Rushmore. The amount is equivalent to $87,721.71 in 2023.

48. South Dakota's official motto is "Under God the people rule."

49. The Oahe Dam in South Dakota creates Lake Oahe, which is the fourth-largest manmade reservoir in the United States.

50. Jewel Cave is 217.32 miles (349.74 kilometers) long and is the fifth longest cave in the world. The only cave longer in America is Mammoth Cave near Brownsville, Kentucky, at almost double the length (426 miles (685.6 kilometers)).

TENNESSEE

1. Tennessee's nickname is the "Volunteer State," in honor of the many volunteers from Tennessee who fought in the War of 1812.

2. Tennessee was named after the Cherokee town of Tanasi, which was in the eastern part of the state prior to the first European-American settlement.

3. Tennessee became the 16th state of the United States on June 1, 1796.

4. Nashville is the capital and largest city of Tennessee.

5. Memphis, Tennessee, is the second-largest city on the Mississippi River and is known for its rich musical heritage. The only city on the Mississippi River that is larger is New Orleans.

6. Tennessee is home to the Great Smoky Mountains National Park. With upwards of 14 million visitors annually, it is the most visited national park in the United States.

7. The Grand Ole Opry is a legendary country music venue in Nashville, Tennessee.

8. Jack Daniel's, a world-famous whiskey, is distilled in Lynchburg, Tennessee.

9. Graceland, the former home of Elvis Presley, is in Memphis and is one of the most visited private homes in the United States.

10. Tennessee is one of only two (Kanas being the other) dry states by default, meaning counties must expressly authorize the sale of alcohol or alcoholic beverages. Tennessee has five dry counties where the sale of alcohol or alcoholic beverages is prohibited or restricted.

11. Tennessee's official state flower is the iris.

12. The Battle of Shiloh was a major battle in the Civil War that took place in southwestern Tennessee.

13. The Nashville sit-ins were a demonstration to end racial segregation that had students occupy lunch counters in downtown Nashville. By the end, more than 150 students were arrested for their part in the sit-ins.

14. The Tennessee Valley Authority (TVA) was created by Congress under Franklin D. Roosevelt's New Deal in 1933 to provide electricity, flood control, and economic development to the Tennessee Valley region.

15. Dollywood in Pigeon Forge, Tennessee, is a theme park co-founded by Dolly Parton.

16. Bristol, Tennessee, is known as the "Birthplace of Country Music" due to the historic 1927 Bristol Sessions recording sessions. The Birthplace of Country Music Museum sits right across the border in Bristol, Virginia, however.

17. The first self-service grocery store in the United States, Piggly Wiggly, opened in Memphis in 1916.

18. As of 2003, Tennessee's official state fruit is the tomato.

19. Oak Ridge, Tennessee, was established as a production site for the Manhattan Project in 1942. The goal of the Manhattan Project was to develop the world's first nuclear weapons. The Manhattan Project was a joint project with Canada and the United Kingdom.

20. Gatlinburg, Tennessee, is a resort town known as the "Gateway to the Smoky Mountains."

21. The Bell Witch Haunting is a famous folklore regarding the 19th-century Bell family of Robertson County, Tennessee.

22. The Racoon has been Tennessee's official wild animal since 1971.

23. The Tennessee Aquarium in Chattanooga, Tennessee, is home to over 10,000 animals and close to 800 different species.

24. The W.C. Handy House in Memphis commemorates the "Father of the Blues."

25. Also known as the Knoxville International Energy Exposition (KIEE), the 1982 World's Fair was held in Knoxville, Tennessee.

26. Tennessee is known for its distinct regions: West, Middle, and East Tennessee.

27. Reelfoot Lake, with an average depth of 5.5 feet (1.7 meters) and a maximum depth of 18 feet (5.5 meters), was formed in northwestern Tennessee due to the 1811-1812 New Madrid earthquakes. Reelfoot Lake is Tennessee's only large natural lake, occupying around 15,000 acres (6,070 hectares).

28. The Battle of Fort Pillow is also known as the "Fort Pillow Massacre" because it "marked one the bleakest, saddest events of American military history." The battle in Lauderdale County, Tennessee, resulted in over 300 American lives being lost.

29. The Tennessee State Capitol in Nashville is designed in the Greek Revival style.

30. The "Scopes Monkey Trial" took place in Dayton, Tennessee, in 1925, in which high school teacher John T. Scopes was tried in a criminal court for teaching human evolution in a state-funded school. Scopes was found guilty and was unsuccessful in his appeal.

31. Battle Above the Clouds, or Battle of Lookout Mountain, was a Civil War battle in Chattanooga, Tennessee.

32. Tennessee's state slogan is "Tennessee—America at Its Best."

33. In 1916, Ernest Holmes Sr. invented the first tow truck in Chattanooga, Tennessee.

34. The Ryman Auditorium in Nashville was the home of the Grand Ole Opry from 1943 to 1974 and the winter venue from 1939 to 2020. The Winter Ryman residency was not revived after the COVID-19 pandemic.

35. Nashville's Centennial Park is home to a full-scale replica of Athens' Parthenon. The model was built in 1897 and functions as an art museum.

36. Lynchburg, Tennessee, where Jack Daniel's whiskey is produced, is in Moore County, a dry county, meaning alcohol sales are prohibited. An exception has been made for purchases on the premises of the Jack Daniel's Distillery.

37. The International Friendship Bell in Oak Ridge, Tennessee, serves as an expression of hope for everlasting peace and friendship between the United States and Japan.

38. Sweetwater, Tennessee, is home to the Craighead Caverns containing the Lost Sea, the largest underground lake in the United States.

39. Gatlinburg is home to the Salt and Pepper Shaker Museum, showcasing over 20,000 pairs.

40. The Bonnaroo Music and Arts Festival takes place in Manchester, Tennessee. It is one of the largest music festivals in the United States, drawing, on average, more than 75,000 attendees each year.

41. The White Squirrel Festival in Kenton, Tennessee, celebrates the town's sizeable albino squirrel population.

42. At 42 feet (12.8 meters) tall, the Athena sculpture, located inside the Nashville Parthenos, is the tallest indoor sculpture in the Western Hemisphere.

43. David Crockett, better known as Davy Crockett, was an American frontiersman, soldier, politician, and folk hero who was born in Tennessee and represented Tennessee in the United States House of Representatives.

44. The first to settle in Tennessee were of French descent.

45. Kingston, Tennessee, was the capital of Tennessee on September 21, 1807, the only day it held that title.

46. Tennessee has more than 10,000 known caves, making it the state that is home to the most caves in the United States. Texas is second with just under 6,000.

47. Martin Luther King Jr. was assassinated at the Lorraine Motel in Memphis, Tennessee, on April 4, 1968.

48. Barney and Ally Harman, Tennessee beverage bottlers, created the original formula for Mountain Dew in 1940 in Knoxville, Tennessee, as a soft drink to mix with liquor.

49. With over 600,000 visitors annually, Graceland is the 2nd most visited home in the United States. Only The White House receives more visitors each year.

50. Tennessee is home to the city of Paris, complete with a 70-foot (21-meter) tall replica of the Eiffel Tower.

TEXAS

1. Texas is known as the "Lone Star State" due to the single star on its flag symbolizing its independent past.

2. Texas is the second-largest state in the United States by both area and population.

3. Texas was an independent country called the Republic of Texas from 1836 to 1845 before joining the United States.

4. Texas has a diverse geography, including deserts, plains, mountains, and coastlines.

5. The capital of Texas is Austin, known for its vibrant music scene.

6. The Alamo in San Antonio is a historic site where a pivotal battle in Texas history took place during the Texas Revolution.

7. The Texas state motto is "Friendship."

8. Houston is the state's largest city and the fourth-largest city in the U.S.

9. The King Ranch in Texas is the largest ranch in the United States. At around 825,000 acres (333,865 hectares), it is larger than the state of Rhode Island.

10. Houston is home to the Houston Space Center, which played a crucial role in the Apollo space program and now serves as a science museum.

11. The San Jacinto Monument rises 567.31 feet (172.92 meters) high. Located in Harris County, Texas, the monument commemorates the site of the Battle of San Jacinto, the decisive battle of the Texas Revolution in 1836 that led to Texas' freedom from Mexican control.

12. Texas is the most diverse state in the United States in terms of butterfly species. Out of the 732 species which have been recorded in North America, over 400 have been recorded in Texas.

13. Texas has the most road bridges in the United States. With 55,701, it has more than double Ohio, which comes in second.

14. Texas' State Capitol Building in Austin is the sixth-tallest state capitol in the United States at 302.64 feet (92.24 meters). It stands taller than the United States Capitol in Washington, D.C.

15. Texas Medical Center is a 2.1-square mile (5.4 km²) medical district with over 60 medical institutions located within. It is the largest medical complex in the world.

16. The Lyndon B. Johnson Space Center in Houston is a complex of 100 buildings on 1,620 acres (655.6 hectares) where NASA's Mission Control Center is located.

17. The state's official tree is the pecan tree.

18. The Dallas-Fort Worth International Airport is the second busiest airport in the world in terms of passenger traffic. Atlanta's Hartsfield-Jackson is the busiest airport in the world.

19. The Rio Grande River forms a natural border between Texas and Mexico.

20. The state has its own unique cuisine, including Tex-Mex and kolaches.

21. The city of Galveston is known for its historic architecture and beachfront attractions.

22. San Antonio is famous for its River Walk, a picturesque network of walkways along the San Antonio River.

23. The state has a significant German heritage, especially in towns like New Braunfels and Fredericksburg.

24. Bracken Cave, outside San Antonio, is home to more than 15 million Mexican free-tailed bats, making it the largest bat colony in the world.

25. The Chisos Mountains in Big Bend National Park are the only mountain range entirely contained within a U.S. national park.

26. The Texas Longhorn is a breed of cattle known for its distinct curved horns.

27. Texas' Palo Duro Canyon is the second-largest canyon in the United States.

28. Marfa, Texas, is known for its strange lights, known as the Marfa Lights. The first sighting of which was in 1883.

29. The Sam Houston Monument in Houston honors the state's first and third president during its time as the Republic of Texas.

30. Padre Island National Seashore is the longest undeveloped barrier island in the world at 70 miles (112.7 kilometers) long.

31. Corpus Christi is home to the USS Lexington, an aircraft carrier turned museum.

32. Amarillo is known for its iconic Cadillac Ranch, featuring buried Cadillacs as a public art installation and sculpture.

33. The world's largest pair of cowboy boots stands in San Antonio at 35 feet (10.67 meters) tall and 33 feet (10.06 meters) long.

34. Dr. Pepper was invented in Waco, Texas, in the 1880s.

35. Luckenbach, Texas, boasts a population of three people and the slogan "Everybody's Somebody in Luckenbach."

36. Austin is home to the annual Eeyore's Birthday Party, a whimsical event celebrating the *Winnie the Pooh* character annually since 1963. Eeyore's birthday is the last Saturday of April.

37. The Houston Astrodome, in Houston, was the world's first multi-purpose, domed sports stadium, earning it the nickname "Eighth Wonder of the World" when it opened in 1965.

38. The "Leaning Tower of Texas" is a water tower in the town of Groom that leans at a deliberate angle.

39. The Rose Garden Center in Tyler, Texas, is home to over 38,000 rose bushes, making it the most extensive collection of roses in the United States.

40. Houston, San Antonio, and Dallas all have populations of more than one million people.

41. Texas' official state flower is the bluebonnet.

42. Texas has been a part of Spain, France, Mexico, the Republic of Texas, The United States, and the Confederate States of America.

43. John F. Kennedy was assassinated in Dallas, Texas.

44. Austin is known as the "Live Music Capital of the World."

45. The Caverns of Sonora in Sonora, Texas, are characterized by their unique calcite crystal formations and helictites.

46. Dallas, Texas, is the birthplace of the frozen margarita.

47. Texas is also home to a city named Paris. Paris, Texas, has its own Eiffel Tower at 65 feet (19.8 meters) tall. Built in 1993, the Texas replica is topped with a red cowboy hat.

48. The cities of Austin, Dallas-Fort Worth, Houston, and San Antonio make up the "Texas Triangle" and has a population of more than seven million people combined.

49. Texas is the 5th largest wine-producing state behind California, Washington, New York, and Oregon.

50. There are more than one million registered guns in Texas, almost twice that of the second-highest state, Florida.

UTAH

1. Utah is known as the "Beehive State" for its symbol of industry and unselfishness.

2. Utah became the 45th state on January 4, 1896.

3. The Great Salt Lake is the largest saltwater lake in the Western Hemisphere.

4. Arches National Park contains over 2,000 natural stone arches, the highest concentration in the world.

5. Utah is home to five national parks: Zion, Bryce Canyon, Capitol Reef, Arches, and Canyonlands. The only states that have more are Alaska and California.

6. The Grand Staircase-Escalante National Monument is a vast area of canyons and cliffs. Due to its remote location, it was the last land to be mapped in the contiguous United States.

7. The Bonneville Salt Flats, a remnant of the Pleistocene Lake Bonneville, are known for land speed record attempts.

8. The Sundance Film Festival in Park City is one of the largest independent film festivals globally.

9. The Spiral Jetty is an iconic earthwork sculpture in the Great Salt Lake. It was constructed in 197 by Robert Smithson.

10. The state's official flower is the sego lily.

11. The Delicate Arch in Arches National Park is an iconic symbol of Utah.

12. Salt Lake City hosted the 2002 Winter Olympics.

13. Utah has a desert climate, but its mountains receive significant snowfall, making it a diverse environment.

14. The Salt Lake Temple, the main Temple of the Church of Jesus Christ of Latter-day Saints, in Salt Lake City, took 40 years to complete. It is the largest Latter-day Saints temple by floor area.

15. The Golden Spike National Historic Site commemorates the completion of the First Transcontinental Railroad. The Central Pacific Railroad and the first Union Pacific Railroad met at the site on May 10, 1869.

16. The state is home to the densest concentration of Jurassic dinosaur fossils in the world, the Cleveland-Lloyd Dinosaur Quarry. Over 15,000 bones have been excavated at the site.

17. The state has a variety of natural bridges, including Rainbow Bridge, which has a span of 275 feet (83.82 meters).

18. Salt Lake City's Temple Square is the spiritual and administrative center of The Church of Jesus Christ of Latter-day Saints.

19. The Great Salt Lake's salinity is much higher than that of the ocean. The lake's salinity fluctuates between five and 27 percent, while the ocean is around 3.5 percent.

20. The Utah State Capitol in Salt Lake City features a distinctive neoclassical revival, Corinthian design.

21. The Uinta Mountains are known for their unique east-west alignment.

22. Utah is home to the Red Fleet State Park, featuring dinosaur footprints.

23. Utah has 38 mountain peaks that exceed 10,000 feet (3,048 meters), five of which exceed 12,000 feet (3657.6 meters).

24. The Bingham Canyon Mine, also known as Kennecott Copper Mine, lies southwest of Salt Lake City and is the largest man-made excavation and deepest open pit mine in the world.

25. The first Kentucky Fried Chicken franchise was opened in Salt Lake City.

26. The town of Kanab is known as Utah's "Little Hollywood" due to its use as a filming location.

27. Moqui marbles, spherical sandstone formations, are found in various parts of Utah.

28. In February 1933, Utah became the 36th state to approve the 21st Amendment. Utah's approval was the deciding vote. The 21st Amendment abolished prohibition.

29. Brigham Young arrived in Utah's Great Salt Lake Valley on July 24, 1847.

30. "Metaphor: The Tree of Utah" is a large sculpture along Interstate 80, resembling a tree with colored spheres as leaves. The sculpture stands 87 feet (26.5 meters) tall.

31. Utah's State Capitol's dome is covered in Utah copper.

32. Utah had been a United States territory since 1850 but was not granted statehood until 1896, when it outlawed polygamy.

33. Zion National Park was once home to the Anasazi people, also known as the Ancestral Puebloans.

34. The Bonneville Salt Flats are the largest salt flats in the United States at over 46 square miles (119 km²) in size.

35. Utah's official state bird is the California Gull.

36. More than 60 percent of Utahns identify as members of The Church of Jesus Christ of Latter-day Saints.

37. Kings Peak is the highest point in Utah. The summit sits at 13,528 feet (4,123 meters) above sea level.

38. Utah has the youngest population by average in the United States. The median age range is around 30 years old, while the median in the United States is about 38 years old.

39. Over 60 percent of Utah is owned by the United States.

40. Utah's official state cooking pot is the Dutch oven. Texas and Arkansas have also given the Dutch oven the honor of being their official state cooking pots.

41. The Great Salt Lake is the eighth-largest terminal lake in the world. A terminal lake or endorheic lake is one with no outlet.

42. Lake Powell is the second largest artificial reservoir by maximum water capacity in the United States. Only Lake Mead in Nevada can hold more water.

43. William DeVries first used the artificial heart for permanent implantation at the University of Utah in 1982. Today, more than 1,700 artificial hearts have helped add years to lives.

44. Fillmore, Utah, was named after President Millard Fillmore. The city was also the capital of the Utah Territory from 1851 to 1856.

45. Provo, Utah, is home to the Missionary Training Centers, which trains Mormon missionaries before embarking on their missions. The missionaries usually spend anywhere from three to 12 weeks at the center. It is the only Missionary Training Center in the United States. However, additional centers exist in England, Ghana, Mexico, Peru, the Philippines, South Africa, New Zealand, and Brazil.

46. Utah is still home to over 30,000 pro-polygamy groups.

47. One of the largest known collections of petroglyphs can be found at the Newspaper Rock State Historic Monument in San Juan County, Utah.

48. The current flag of the State of Utah was adopted in 2011.

49. There is over four billion tons of salt dissolved in the Great Salt Lake.

50. Granite Mountain in Utah has a secret vault located inside the mountain. The vault, known as the Granite Mountain Records Vault, holds the most extensive collection of genealogical records in the world and is owned by the Church of Jesus Christ of Latter-day Saints.

VERMONT

1. Vermont is known as "The Green Mountain State."

2. Vermont is the second least populous state in the United States.

3. The state capital is Montpelier, which is the smallest state capital by population in the U.S.

4. Vermont is known for its picturesque landscapes, including rolling hills, forests, and lakes.

5. Vermont is famous for its vibrant fall foliage, attracting tourists from around the world.

6. The state motto is "Freedom and unity."

7. Vermont was the 14th state to join the Union on March 4, 1791.

8. The Bread and Puppet Theater, known for its political performances, was founded in Vermont.

9. Ben & Jerry's, a well-known ice cream company, was founded in Vermont.

10. In 1777, Vermont became the first state to abolish adult slavery.

11. Burlington, Vermont, is the most populous city in the state, the smallest most populous city of any state.

12. Vermont is home to the largest underground marble quarry in the world.

13. The Long Trail, running 273 miles (439 meters), is the oldest long-distance trail in the United States. Being constructed between 1910 and 1930, the Long Trail runs the length of the state.

14. Vermont has no billboards, which contributes to its scenic beauty.

15. The Trapp Family Lodge in Stowe, Vermont, is a resort famously owned by the von Trapp Family of *The Sound of Music* fame.

16. Vermont's Green Mountains are a part of the Appalachian Mountain range.

17. Vermont has a strong tradition of town meetings where residents gather to make local decisions. The town meetings take place on the first Tuesday in March every year.

18. Burlington, Vermont, is home to "File Under So. Co., Waiting for...," an art installation of a filing cabinet over 40 feet (12 meters) tall.

19. The Hubbardton Battlefield marks the site of the only Revolutionary War battle fought in Vermont.

20. Vermont only has ten cities but has 237 towns.

21. Vermont's state bird is the hermit thrush.

22. The Ethan Allen Homestead Museum commemorates the life of the Revolutionary War hero Ethan Allen, who was the leader of the Green Mountain Boys.

23. The Vermont State Fair, held in Rutland since 1846, is one of the oldest state fairs in the country.

24. The Dog Chapel in St. Johnsbury, Vermont, is a unique chapel that celebrates the spiritual bond between humans and dogs, created by artist Stephen Huneck.

25. Wilson Castle in Proctor, Vermont, is a unique 19th-century estate that mixes Dutch neo-renaissance, Scottish baronial, Queen Anne, and Romanesque Revival architecture.

26. Barre, Vermont, is known for its granite quarries, proclaiming itself the "Granite Center of the World."

27. Vermont's state mammal is the Morgan horse.

28. The Vermont Symphony Orchestra is one of the few state-supported symphony orchestras in the United States. It also holds the distinction of being the oldest such orchestra.

29. The Vermont state tree is the sugar maple, which is closely tied to the maple syrup industry.

30. The Ethan Allen Express is a train route connecting Vermont to New York City. The trip is 310 miles (499 kilometers) and takes around seven and one-half hours.

31. From 1777 to 1791, Vermont was known as the Vermont Republic.

32. The town of Waterbury is home to the Ben & Jerry's Flavor Graveyard, where discontinued ice cream flavors are "buried."

33. The Haskell Free Library and Opera House straddles the U.S.-Canada border, allowing visitors to see a show in one country and read in the other. The only entrance is on the United States side.

However, Canadians are permitted to enter through a particular path without needing to pass through customs.

34. Vermont produces over two million gallons of maple syrup each year, the most of any state.

35. Vermont was the first state to introduce "civil unions" for same-sex couples in 2000, paving the way for marriage equality.

36. Vermont has an annual "Flannel Day," encouraging people to wear flannel clothing to work or school.

37. Vermont has more than 100 covered bridges, giving it more covered bridges per square mile than any other state in the United States.

38. Vermont's state capitol building, the Vermont State House, is topped by a statue of Ceres, the Roman goddess of agriculture.

39. The first-ever U.S. patent was issued in 1790 to Samuel Hopkins of Vermont for a process of making potash, used in soap and glass production.

40. The tallest building in Vermont, Decker Towers, is only 11 stories high and comes in at 124 feet (37.8 meters) tall.

41. Vermont's name is derived from French. "Ver" comes from "vert," meaning green, and "mont" from "montagne" meaning mountain. The name literally translates to "green mountain."

42. Montpelier, Vermont, is the only state capital without a McDonald's.

43. Vermont's official state animal is the Morgan horse, which was one of the earliest breeds developed in the United States. The U.S.

Morgan Horse Farm was originally in Middlebury, Vermont, before being moved to the University of Vermont.

44. Vermont offers snowboarding in high school as a varsity sport with a state championship—one of only two states to do so.

45. Lake Champlain was technically the sixth Great Lake for 18 days in 1998.

46. Vermont has been a part of New York and New Hampshire in the past.

47. Vermont has the most breweries per capita, with around one brewery per every 140 square miles (362 km²).

48. The town of Brattleboro hosts the world's first and only "Strolling of the Heifers" parade. The parade is the opposite of the Running of the Bulls, with groomed heifers being casually walked down the street.

49. The town of Barre is home to the E. L. Smith Quarry, the world's largest "deep hole" granite quarry.

50. Vermont's state wildflower is the red clover, a common and vibrant flowering plant found throughout the state.

VIRGINIA

1. Virginia is known as the "Mother of Presidents" because it is the birthplace of eight U.S. presidents.

2. Virginia's state's nickname is the "Old Dominion."

3. Virginia was one of the original 13 colonies.

4. The city of Richmond is the capital.

5. The first permanent English settlement in North America was Jamestown, Virginia, in 1607.

6. The "Virginia is for Lovers" slogan was created in 1969 as part of a tourism campaign.

7. Arlington, Virginia, is home to the Pentagon, the headquarters of the U.S. Department of Defense.

8. The Chesapeake Bay Bridge was the world's longest continuous over-water steel structure when it opened in 1952. The bridge is over 4.3 miles (6.9 kilometers) long and connects Virginia's Eastern Shore to the Western Shore.

9. Virginia's state flower and state tree is the Flowering Dogwood.

10. George Washington, the 1st president of the United States, was born in Westmoreland County, Virginia.

11. Virginia Beach is known for having one of the longest pleasure beaches in the world.

12. The University of Virginia in Charlottesville was founded by Thomas Jefferson over 200 years ago in 1819.

13. The first fraternity, Phi Beta Kappa, began at the College of William & Mary in Williamsburg, Virginia.

14. Arlington National Cemetery, located in Arlington County, Virginia, is a burial site for military personnel and notable figures. Arlington National Cemetery is home to almost 400,000 burial sites and is one of two cemeteries in the United States National Cemetery System.

15. The Pentagon is the second largest office building in the world. The Pentagon has over 6.5 million square feet (600,000 square meters) of floor space.

16. Virginia's state motto is "Sic semper tyrannis," which means "Thus Always to Tyrants."

17. The College of William & Mary in Williamsburg is the second-oldest institution of higher education in the United States. Founded in 1693, it was the first college to become a university in 1779.

18. Kentucky and West Virginia used to be part of Virginia.

19. The "Virginia Declaration of Rights," drafted in 1776, influenced the U.S. Bill of Rights, which was drafted in 1789.

20. The Colonial Williamsburg historic district offers a glimpse into 18th-century life in Virginia.

21. The Virginia State Capitol in Richmond was designed by Thomas Jefferson and Charles-Louis Clérisseau.

22. The National D-Day Memorial in Bedford, Virginia, honors the sacrifices made on D-Day during World War II.

23. Norfolk, Virginia, is home to the world's largest naval base, Naval Station Norfolk.

24. Having opened in 1933, the Barter Theatre in Abingdon, Virginia, is the longest-running professional theater in the United States.

25. Virginia's official state fossil is the *Chesapecten jeffersonius*, named after Thomas Jefferson.

26. The "USS Wisconsin," a battleship, is permanently moored at Nauticus, a maritime-themed museum and science center in Norfolk.

27. The current Virginia State Capitol Building in Richmond is the eighth built to serve this purpose. Multiple have been lost to fires.

28. Monticello, Thomas Jefferson's primary residence, is a UNESCO World Heritage Site.

29. The Jamestown Settlement in Jamestown, Virginia, was created in 1957 and is a living history museum showcasing the early colonial period.

30. The Chesapeake Bay is the largest estuary in the United States and a crucial ecosystem.

31. The state's official boat is the Chesapeake Bay Deadrise, a traditional fishing boat.

32. The Luray Caverns in Luray are some of the largest and most well-known caverns in the eastern United States.

33. The Pentagon, located in Arlington County, Virginia, has six different ZIP codes, all of which are Washington D.C. ZIP codes. The four service branches, the Joint Chiefs of Staff, and the U.S. Secretary of Defense, all have their own ZIP codes.

34. The Manassas National Battlefield Park preserves the site of two significant Civil War battles. The First Battle of Bull Run (also called the Battle of First Manassas) and the Second Battle of Bull Run (also called the Battle of Second Manassas).

35. The "Chincoteague Pony Swim" involves herding wild ponies from Assateague Island to Chincoteague Island by swimming across the channel. The tradition began in 1924.

36. Bristol, Virginia, and Bristol, Tennessee, share a state line down their main street, State Street.

37. Mount Vernon in Fairfax County, Virginia, is known for being the site of George Washington's home.

38. The town of Natural Bridge in Rockbridge County, Virginia, features a massive natural limestone arch standing 215 feet (65.5 meters) tall with a span of 90 feet (27 meters).

39. The town of Galax is known as the "center of traditional 'old-time' music and musicians." A title it shares with Round Peak, North Carolina, located around 15 miles (24 kilometers) away.

40. Virginia's state bat, the Virginia Big-eared Bat, plays a crucial role in insect control. The bat is known for its large ears; while only around four inches in total length, the bat's ears can measure around 1.25 inches in length.

41. Northern Virginia is the "data capital of the world" and is home to over 30 percent of the world's hyperscale data centers.

42. Virginia has a "Stonehenge " replica in Centreville, known as "Foamhenge," made entirely of foam. Foamhenge was originally in Natural Bridge, Virginia, but was moved in 2017.

43. The largest state park in Virginia is Pocahontas State Park in Chesterfield County, Virginia.

44. The mouth of the Chesapeake Bay is home to the Chesapeake Bay impact crater, a buried impact crater that collided with the eastern shore in the late Eocene epoch, around about 35.5 ± 0.3 million years ago.

45. Virginia is named after Queen Elizabeth I of England, who was known as the "Virgin Queen."

46. Smithfield hams can only come from the town of Smithfield, in Isle of Wight County, in the Hampton Roads region of Virginia.

47. Thomas Jefferson, the 3rd president of the United States, died in Charlottesville, Virginia, on July 4, 1826, the same exact day that John Adams, the 2nd president of the United States, died in Quincy, Massachusetts.

48. Virginia Beach is the most populous city in Virginia, with over 400,000 inhabitants.

49. ChapStick was invented by pharmacist Dr. Charles Browne Fleet in 1869 in Lynchburg, Virginia.

50. During the American Civil War, Richmond, Virginia, and Danville, Virginia, both served as the capitals of the Confederacy at different points. The only other city to hold that title was Montgomery, Alabama.

WASHINGTON

1. Washington's unofficial state nickname is "The Evergreen State" due to its lush green landscapes.

2. Seattle is the largest city in Washington and is known for its tech industry, including companies like Microsoft and Amazon.

3. Washington was named after George Washington, the first President of the United States.

4. Washington is home to the Hoh Rainforest, located on the Olympic Peninsula, one of the largest temperate rainforests in the United States.

5. The Space Needle in Seattle was built for the 1962 World's Fair and has become an iconic symbol of the city. Once the tallest structure west of the Mississippi River, the Space Needle stands 605 feet (184 meters) tall.

6. Washington is the birthplace of Starbucks, which opened its first store in Seattle in 1971. Starbucks is the world's largest coffeehouse chain.

7. Mount Rainier is the highest peak in the state, with a summit elevation of 14,417 feet (4,394 meters) and an active stratovolcano.

8. Washington is the leading producer of hops in the United States, with over 65% of the hops in the United States being produced there.

9. Washington is home to four floating bridges. There are only 20 floating bridges in the world, of which four of the five longest are in Washington.

10. The Columbia River Gorge is a stunning natural area that forms a border between Washington and Oregon.

11. The San Juan Islands offer beautiful landscapes and are a popular whale-watching destination.

12. Washington's state flag features the state seal, a portrait of George Washington, on a field of dark green with the words "The Seal of the State of Washington" above and below with the date 1889.

13. The Boeing Company, one of the world's largest aerospace manufacturers, was founded in Seattle.

14. Olympia is the state capital of Washington.

15. Spokane, Washington, hosts the largest three-on-three basketball tournament in the world, called Hoopfest. The tournament draws in more than 6,000 teams and more than 200,000 fans.

16. Washington has a diverse range of ecosystems, from coastal areas to mountains and forests.

17. The Grand Coulee Dam on the Columbia River is one of the largest concrete structures in the world and the largest power station in the United States in terms of rated capacity at 6,809 megawatts.

18. Washington was the 42nd state admitted to the Union in 1889.

19. The state's official marine mammal is the Orca Whale, commonly known as the killer whale.

20. The state's motto is "Alki," which means "by and by" in Chinook Jargon.

21. Washington is the second leading producer of wine in the United States after California.

22. The Chihuly Garden and Glass in Seattle showcases the breathtaking glass artwork of Dale Chihuly.

23. The city of Spokane was initially named "Spokane Falls" after the waterfalls of the Spokane River located in downtown Spokane.

24. Washington is the largest producer of apples, pears, blueberries, and sweet cherries in the United States.

25. The Museum of Flight in Seattle houses an extensive collection of aircraft and aerospace artifacts. The private non-profit air and space museum is the largest in the world.

26. The Palouse region is known for its rolling hills and is a major wheat-producing area.

27. The Washington State Ferries system maintains the largest fleet of ferries in the United States. The ferries service 20 terminals around Puget Sound and the San Juan Islands.

28. The Fremont Troll, a public art installation, resides under the Aurora Avenue Bridge in Seattle. The sculpture was introduced in 1990 and is 18 feet (5.5 meters) high.

29. Washington is the only state named after a U.S. president. The state was named after George Washington.

30. The Boeing Everett Factory, located in Everett, Washington, is the largest building in the world by volume at 13,385,378 m3 (472,370,319 cu ft). The factory covers 98.7 acres (39.9 hectares) and employs over 30,000 people.

31. Washington is home to more than 3,000 alpine glaciers—the second most of any state after Alaska.

32. Seattle is famous for its frequent rainfall, earning the nickname "Rain City."

33. Pike Place Market in Seattle, Washington, opened on August 17, 1907, making it one of the oldest continuously operated public farmers' markets in the United States.

34. The city of Spokane hosted the first environmentally-themed World's Fair in 1974, known as Expo '74.

35. The Olympic National Park features three distinct ecosystems: subalpine forest and wildflower meadow, temperate forest, and coastline.

36. The Sasquatch! music festival in George, Washington, draws thousands of music lovers each year.

37. The "World's Largest Egg" statue stands in Winlock, symbolizing the town's egg production. The egg is 12 feet (3.66 meters) long and weighs 1,200 pounds (544 kilograms).

38. The Leavenworth Nutcracker Museum in Leavenworth, Washington, houses over 9,000 nutcrackers from over 50 countries.

39. Washington's official state vegetable is the Walla Walla Sweet Onion, known for its mild flavor.

40. The town of Sequim, Washington, is known as the "Lavender Capital of North America" and hosts an annual lavender festival.

41. The Fremont neighborhood in Seattle is home to a statue of Vladimir Lenin. The figure is 16 feet (5.33 meters) tall and cast in bronze.

42. Washington's official state ship is the Lady Washington, a replica of an 18th-century sailing vessel. The ship calls Aberdeen, Washington home.

43. Bickleton, Washington, is known as the bluebird capital of the world.

44. Evergreen Point Floating Bridge is the longest floating bridge in the world, spanning 7,710 feet (2,350 meters). The bridge is also the widest in the world at 116 feet (35 meters).

45. The Columbia River was named after Captain Robert Gray's ship, *Columbia Rediviva*. The ship was the first American vessel to circumnavigate the globe.

46. The Nutty Narrows Bridge is a 60-foot (18.3 meter) long suspension bridge in Longview, Washington, that was built in 1963 for squirrels, making it easier for them to cross the street without being hit by cars. Longview is home to eight squirrel bridges.

47. Father's Day was first celebrated in Spokane, Washington, in 1910 by Sonora Smart Dodd.

48. Washington is home to 29 federally recognized Native American tribes.

49. More than half of the United States apple production is from Washington state.

50. Point Roberts, Washington, can only be accessed by land through Canada.

WEST VIRGINIA

1. West Virginia's nickname is the "Mountain State" due to its rugged terrain.

2. West Virginia was formed during the Civil War as a separate state from Virginia in 1863.

3. West Virginia is the only state entirely within the Appalachian Region.

4. The state's motto is "Montani semper liberi," meaning "Mountaineers are always free."

5. Charleston is the capital and most populous city of West Virginia.

6. The New River Gorge Bridge is the world's fifth-longest single-span arch bridge. The bridge spans 1,700 feet (518 meters) and was the longest in the world when it opened in 1977.

7. The first 4-H camp in the world was held in Randolph County, West Virginia.

8. Harpers Ferry was the site of John Brown's raid on the U.S. Armory in 1859.

9. The state is a popular destination for white-water rafting, particularly on the Gauley River.

10. West Virginia is the only state to form by separating from a Confederate state.

11. At around 97 percent, West Virginia has the highest percentage of Caucasians in the United States.

12. The Golden Delicious apple, a popular variety, was discovered in Clay County, West Virginia.

13. The first Mother's Day was observed in Grafton, West Virginia, in 1907. Anna Jarvis held a memorial service at her late mother's church on May 12. In 1914, President Woodrow Wilson made it a national holiday.

14. West Virginia is known for its bluegrass and Appalachian music traditions.

15. The West Virginia State Penitentiary in Moundsville is known for its haunted history and offers tours.

16. West Virginia has a rich coal mining history and was once a major coal-producing region.

17. The West Virginia State Capitol building features a dome covered in copper and gold leaf.

18. Mothman, a legendary creature, is said to have been sighted in Point Pleasant.

19. Shepherdstown, established in 1762, is one of the oldest towns in West Virginia and is known for its historic charm.

20. The West Virginia Strawberry Festival has been celebrated annually since 1936 in Buckhannon.

21. The Allegheny Front is a prominent geological feature running through the state.

22. Berkeley Springs is known for its historic mineral springs and is often called "America's First Spa."

23. The pepperoni roll, a popular local snack, originated in West Virginia.

24. The West Virginia Independence Hall in Wheeling is a National Historic Landmark and is currently a state-run museum.

25. The Green Bank Observatory in Pocahontas County is home to the world's largest fully steerable radio telescope.

26. West Virginia is home to the Mystery Hole attraction, where gravity seems to defy the rules.

27. The town of Thurmond has a population of just five people but boasts a historic train depot. It is the second least-used station in Amtrak's network of over 500 stations.

28. In White Sulphur Springs, the Greenbrier Resort is home to a once-secret government bunker.

29. West Virginia's Eastern Panhandle is part of the Washington-Baltimore-Arlington metropolitan area.

30. West Virginia is home to a number of unique covered bridges, including the Philippi Covered Bridge. The Philippi Covered Bridge was constructed in 1852 and is the oldest and longest-covered bridge in West Virginia.

31. West Virginia's Trans-Allegheny Lunatic Asylum offers ghost tours and paranormal investigations.

32. The West Virginia Dandelion Festival in White Sulphur Springs celebrates the hardy plant.

33. The Oglebay Festival of Lights in Wheeling is one of the nation's largest Christmas light displays.

34. The state's official state dog is the Appalachian Brood Hound, known for its friendly nature.

35. More than 75 percent of West Virginia is woodland.

36. West Virginia University was known as the Agricultural College of West Virginia for one year.

37. The capital of West Virginia was originally Wheeling until 1870. It then moved to Charleston for five years until it returned to Wheeling. In 1885, Charleston was once again the capital and has remained so since.

38. Charles Town, West Virginia, was named after Charles Washington, George Washington's younger brother.

39. Berkeley Springs State Park is home to George Washington's Bathtub.

40. No dinosaur fossils have ever been found in West Virginia.

41. On May 3, 1921, West Virginia became the first state to enact a sales tax.

42. The Trans-Allegheny Lunatic Asylum's main building is the largest hand-cut stone masonry building in the United States.

43. Cecil H. Underwood became the youngest Governor of West Virginia when he took office in 1957; he was 34 years old. He subsequently became the oldest Governor of West Virginia when he took office for a second term in 1997 at the age of 74.

44. Summers Street in Charleston, West Virginia, was home to the first brick-paved street section in the world in 1870.

45. West Virginia is home to towns named after cities in other countries, including Calcutta, Shanghai, and Berlin.

46. Williamson, West Virginia, is home to the Coal House, a building built of coal masonry.

47. Rural free delivery, a program to deliver mail directly to rural destinations, began in West Virginia in 1896.

48. Morgantown, the third most populous city in West Virginia, becomes the most populous city in West Virginia when the West Virginia University Mountaineers football team plays at Milan Puskar Stadium.

49. The American black bear is the official state mammal of West Virginia.

50. Charleston, the most populous city in West Virginia, has a population of under 50,000.

WISCONSIN

1. Wisconsin is known as the "Badger State" due to lead miners who lived in tunnels for extended periods of time, similar to badgers.

2. Wisconsin's state motto is "Forward."

3. Wisconsin is the dairy capital of the United States, producing cheese, milk, and other dairy products.

4. Milwaukee, the largest city in the state, is famous for its brewing heritage.

5. Door County, known as the "Cape Cod of the Midwest," offers beautiful waterfront views and cherry orchards along the 70-mile (112.7-kilometer) long peninsula.

6. Wisconsin's state dance is the polka, reflecting its strong Polish heritage.

7. The first capital of the Wisconsin Territory was Belmont, Wisconsin.

8. Milwaukee, Wisconsin, is home to the Harley-Davidson Museum and houses more than 450 motorcycles.

9. The House on the Rock, an unusual attraction located between the cities of Spring Green and Dodgeville, features collections of eclectic and bizarre objects.

10. The Ice Age National Scenic Trail runs 1,200 miles (1,931 kilometers) through Wisconsin, showcasing glacial landscapes.

11. The Hodag, a mythical creature, is the official symbol of Rhinelander, Wisconsin.

12. In 1837, the first capitol building in Madison, Wisconsin, was constructed of stone cut from Maple Bluff and locally cut oak.

13. The Milwaukee Art Museum features a unique moving sunscreen called the Burke Brise Soleil, or "wings."

14. Milwaukee is home to Summerfest, one of the largest music festivals in the world.

15. Wisconsin has a strong tradition of Friday night fish fries, a popular dining experience.

16. Wisconsin's official state animal is the badger.

17. Wisconsin is famous for its supper clubs, offering classic American cuisine and cozy atmospheres. Currently, there are over 250 registered supper clubs in the state.

18. Christopher Latham Sholes invented the first practical typewriter in Milwaukee in 1867.

19. The National Mustard Museum in Middleton showcases thousands of mustard varieties from around the world.

20. The EAA AirVenture Oshkosh is the world's largest general aviation event, drawing thousands of aircraft enthusiasts.

21. The current Capitol Building in Madison is the third in the city and was completed in 1917.

22. Wisconsin's official fruit is the cranberry.

23. Wisconsin is home to more than 15,000 lakes.

24. A piece of Sputnik 4, a USSR satellite weighing seven tons, crashed in Manitowoc, Wisconsin on September 5, 1962. A metal ring marks the location of the impact.

25. Milwaukee is home to one of the largest German festivals in North America. German Fest draws thousands of visitors annually on the last full weekend in July.

26. The Dickeyville Grotto in Dickeyville features intricate religious sculptures made of stone and glass.

27. The Mitchell Park Horticultural Conservatory in Milwaukee is known as "The Domes" and is a living museum with plants from around the world.

28. Legislation prohibits any buildings in Madison from being taller than the columns surrounding the dome of the Wisconsin State Capitol. The columns stand at 187 feet (57 meters) tall.

29. Racine is known for its Danish pastries and hosts the annual Kringle Festival.

30. The National Railroad Museum in Ashwaubenon, Wisconsin, showcases historic trains and artifacts. The museum is one of the largest and oldest rail museums in the United States.

31. Although Wisconsin does not border an ocean, Manitowoc is home to the Wisconsin Maritime Museum and the USS Cobia submarine.

32. The Baraboo Hills are known for their unique geology and outdoor recreational opportunities.

33. The Mars Cheese Castle in Kenosha is a quirky shop dedicated to all things cheese.

34. The Apostle Islands National Lakeshore features stunning sea caves along Lake Superior.

35. The International Crane Foundation in Baraboo, Wisconsin, focuses on the conservation of cranes and their habitats.

36. The Milwaukee County Zoo is home to over 3,000 animals from around the world and covers an area of 190 acres (76.9 hectares). The Zoo is home to one of the largest groups of bonobos in one location outside of the Democratic Republic of the Congo, their native home.

37. Located in Dodge County, Wisconsin, the Horicon Marsh State Wildlife Area is the largest cattail marsh in the United States.

38. The World's Largest Brat Fest takes place annually in Madison, celebrating the popular sausage.

39. Wisconsin is known for the World's Largest Six-Pack, a collection of six beer storage tanks made to resemble a six-pack of beer in La Crosse.

40. Elroy, Wisconsin, is famous for its Elroy-Sparta State Trail, the first rail trail in the United States, which opened in 1967.

41. The Kohler-Andrae State Park features sand dunes, a beach, and hiking trails along Lake Michigan.

42. The town of Neillsville is home to the Highground Veterans Memorial Park, featuring a large-scale replica of the Liberty Bell that visitors can ring.

43. The World Championship Snowmobile Derby takes place in Eagle River on the thirst weekend in January. The event began in 1964.

44. In Stevens Point, the World's Largest Trivia Contest is held annually, lasting 54 hours straight.

45. Dr. Evermor's Forevertron sculpture park in Sumpter, Wisconsin, features a collection of recycled industrial artifacts. The sculpture is the world's second-largest scrap metal sculpture at 50 feet (15 meters) high and 120 feet (36.6 meters) wide.

46. Sheboygan is known as the Freshwater Surf Capital of the World.

47. The Green Bay Packers are the only non-profit publicly owned major professional sports franchise in the United States. The franchise has more than 530,000 shareholders.

48. The first Harley-Davidson motorcycle was built in Milwaukee in 1903 by Walter Davidson, Arthur Davidson, William Davidson, and William Harley.

49. The Wisconsin Concrete Park in Phillips, Wisconsin, is home to 237 concrete and mixed media sculptures built by Fred Smith between 1948 and 1964.

50. Senator Gaylord Anton Nelson of Wisconsin introduced the idea of a nationwide environmental teach-in in 1970. The event became what is known today as Earth Day.

WYOMING

1. The state is often called the "Equality State" due to its early recognition of women's suffrage.

2. Wyoming was the 44th state to join the United States.

3. Yellowstone National Park, the first national park in the world, is mainly located in Wyoming.

4. Wyoming has the lowest population of all U.S. states despite it being the 10th largest in terms of area.

5. Cheyenne is the capital and largest city of Wyoming.

6. The state's nickname is the "Cowboy State."

7. Wyoming is famous for its wide-open spaces and natural beauty.

8. Grand Teton National Park is known for its stunning mountain landscape.

9. Devils Tower, a unique rock formation, was designated the first United States national monument in 1906 by President Theodore Roosevelt.

10. The Oregon Trail passed through Wyoming during westward expansion.

11. The Wind River Range is home to Gannett Peak, the highest peak in Wyoming at 13,810 feet (4,209 meters).

12. Wyoming is home to the largest hot springs in the United States, located in Thermopolis.

13. The state's official flower is the Wyoming Indian paintbrush.

14. The Wyoming State Capitol building in Cheyenne is known for its distinctive dome and Renaissance Revival architecture.

15. Fossil Butte National Monument contains some of the world's best-preserved fossils of Cenozoic aquatic communities.

16. There are over 100 named mountain ranges in Wyoming.

17. Wyoming has the second lowest population density after Alaska.

18. The Wind River Range has more than 1,300 named lakes.

19. The Wyoming Territorial Prison, a former federal government prison, is now a historic site and museum located in Laramie, Wyoming.

20. Wyoming has a rich history of mining for coal, uranium, and other minerals.

21. Jackson is often called the "Gateway to Yellowstone."

22. The Shoshone National Forest is one of the world's first nationally protected land areas. The area became protected under President Benjamin Harrison in 1891.

23. Wyoming was the first state to grant women the right to vote in 1869.

24. The University of Wyoming, located in Laramie, is the state's only public four-year university.

25. Fort Laramie, a significant 19th-century trading post, was initially known as Fort William before changing its name to Fort John and finally to Fort Laramie.

26. The state has a strong tradition of rodeos, with the Cheyenne Frontier Days being a major event held annually since 1897 in Cheyenne, Wyoming.

27. Fetterman Battlefield is the site of the United States Army's second-worst defeat. The battle between the U.S. Army and Plains Indians groups saw the death of 81 U.S. soldiers in less than 30 minutes.

28. Vedauwoo, a unique rock formation in Buford, Wyoming, is popular for rock climbing and hiking.

29. Wyoming is home to the National Museum of Wildlife Art in Jackson.

30. The Wyoming State Archives holds historical records dating back to the 1860s and includes more than 500,000 images.

31. The Wyoming Territorial Prison once housed notorious outlaws such as Butch Cassidy.

32. Wyoming's early economy was centered around fur trading and trapping.

33. Fort Laramie National Historic Site preserves an important 19th-century military outpost, trading post, and diplomatic site.

34. Medicine Wheel National Historic Landmark is a Native American archaeological site and Native American sacred complex.

35. The Ames Monument, a pyramid in Albany County, Wyoming, is dedicated to the Union Pacific Railroad's financiers, Oakes Ames and Oliver Ames Jr.

36. The town of Cody is named after the legendary showman Buffalo Bill Cody.

37. The Bridger-Teton National Forest is the third largest national forest in the United States, consisting of 3.4 million acres (13,759 square kilometers).

38. The Heart Mountain Relocation Center between Cody and Powell, Wyoming, was an internment camp for Japanese Americans during World War II.

39. There are more than 40 peaks in the Wind River Range with a height exceeding 13,000 feet (3,962 meters) in elevation.

40. The Jackalope, a mythical creature with the body of a rabbit and antlers of an antelope, is a popular icon in Wyoming and originates in Douglas, Wyoming.

41. The town of Buford, Wyoming, was once touted as the smallest town in America, with a population of just one person—the sole resident left in 2012.

42. Jackson Hole Airport, nestled between mountain ranges, is known for having one of the shortest commercial runways in the U.S.

43. The state is home to the historic Smith Mansion, a unique home that's also a local landmark.

44. The mysterious "Sinks Canyon" features a river that disappears into a cavern, only to reemerge later downstream.

45. At 2.2 million acres (8,903 square kilometers), the Wind River Indian Reservation is the seventh-largest American Indian reservation in the United States.

46. Wyoming has fewer people than Washington, D.C.

47. Wyoming has more active geyser fields than any other state.

48. The town of Kemmerer is home to the first J.C. Penney store, established in 1902 by James Cash Penney.

49. Shoshone National Forest is within the borders of Yellowstone National Park.

50. Grand Teton is one of the youngest mountain ranges in the United States and was formed by a series of earthquakes around 10 million years ago.

WASHINGTON D.C.

1. Washington, D.C., is not a state but a federal district.

2. Washington, D.C., is often called simply D.C.

3. Washington, D.C., was named after George Washington, the United States' first president.

4. The White House, located at 1600 Pennsylvania Avenue, is the official residence and workplace of the president.

5. Contrary to the common usage of the name "mall," The National Mall is not a mall made up of stores but rather a large open area with iconic landmarks and memorials.

6. The Washington Monument is an iconic obelisk that honors George Washington.

7. Washington, D.C., is home to the Smithsonian Institution, a complex of museums and research institutions.

8. The United States Capitol houses the legislative branch of the U.S. government.

9. The city and many of its street grids were designed by Pierre Charles L'Enfant around 1791.

10. Washington, D.C., was established as the capital in 1790.

11. Congress' first session was held in Washington, D.C. in 1800.

12. The Library of Congress has over 173 million cataloged items. It is believed to be the most extensive library in the world in terms of cataloged items (the British Library in London and Boston Spa estimates their collection to be between 170 and 200 million items, but there is no definitive number, rather a 30 million item range).

13. The Lincoln Memorial honors Abraham Lincoln and features his statue. The statue is made of 29 pieces of Georgia white marble and stands 19 feet (5.8 meters) tall.

14. The Martin Luther King Jr. Memorial in West Potomac Park celebrates the civil rights leader. It includes the *Stone of Hope*, consisting of fourteen quotes from Dr. Martin Luther King Jr. as inscriptions.

15. Washington, D.C., has no representation in the U.S. Senate but has a non-voting delegate in the House of Representatives.

16. The area that makes up Washington, D.C., was initially carved out of parts of Maryland and Virginia.

17. The National Gallery of Art houses an extensive collection of artworks.

18. The U.S. Supreme Court, the highest court in the country, is in Washington, D.C.

19. The National Zoo is famous for its giant pandas. The pandas are on loan from the Chinese government. Currently, the National Zoo's

giant pandas will be returned to China by December 7, 2023, with no current plan for loaning Pandas to the United States in the near future.

20. Washington, D.C., is divided into four quadrants: Northwest, Northeast, Southwest, and Southeast.

21. The Height Buildings Act of 1910, passed by the 61st Congress, imposed a height restriction on buildings in residential areas to 90 feet (27 meters). For Commercial areas, the restriction is set at 130 feet (39.6 meters), or the width of the right-of-way of the street of which the building fronts, whichever is shorter.

22. Georgetown is one of the oldest neighborhoods in Washington, D.C., was founded in 1751, and is known for its historic charm.

23. The National Museum of Natural History is the most visited natural history museum in the world.

24. The National Cherry Blossom Festival celebrates the gift of Japanese cherry trees, a gift from the Mayor of Tokyo City, Yukio Ozaki, in 1912.

25. The Washington, D.C. Metro is the third-busiest rapid transit system in the U.S.

26. The Watergate complex is known for the political scandal that led to President Nixon's resignation.

27. Ford's Theatre, which opened in 1863, is where John Wilkes Booth assassinated President Abraham Lincoln on April 14, 1865.

28. The National Cathedral, or the Cathedral Church of Saint Peter and Paul in the City and Diocese of Washington, is the third-largest building in Washington, D.C., and the second-largest church building in the United States.

29. The Tidal Basin, a man-made reservoir covering 107 acres (43 hectares), is a popular spot for walking and enjoying the cherry blossoms.

30. The World War II Memorial, consisting of 56 pillars that represent U.S. States and territories, honors those who served in the armed forces during WWII.

31. The Frederick Douglass National Historic Site preserves the home of the abolitionist Frederick Douglass.

32. Washington, D.C.'s Emancipation Day, celebrated on April 16, marks the end of slavery in the district in 1862.

33. The FBI headquarters, located in the J. Edgar Hoover Building, is in Washington, D.C.

34. The Washington National Cathedral has a Darth Vader grotesque. A grotesque is a carved stone figure, similar to a gargoyle, but without a body figure or a water spout through the mouth.

35. The Smithsonian Institution operates 11 museums, four galleries, and a zoo in Washington, D.C.

36. The International Spy Museum is dedicated to espionage and intelligence.

37. Washington, D.C., is home to the oldest Roman Catholic institution of higher education in the United States, Georgetown University, which was founded by Bishop John Carroll in 1789.

38. The Marine Barracks Washington, D.C., having been established in 1801, is the oldest active post in the Marine Corps.

39. The National Museum of the American Indian is devoted to the cultures and histories of Native American peoples.

40. The Eastern Shore of the Potomac River is part of the district's territory.

41. Washington, D.C.'s official flower is the American Beauty rose.

42. The Albert Einstein Memorial, near the National Academy of Sciences, honors the physicist.

43. The International Monetary Fund (IMF) and the World Bank are headquartered in Washington, D.C.

44. There are 23 different federal police agencies in Washington, D.C., with a uniformed presence in the area, including the United States Capitol Police, the United States Secret Service, and the Supreme Court of the United States Police.

45. The Zero Milestone is a monument in Washington, D.C., which was intended to measure the distance of all roads in the United States from a single starting point. However, only the roads in Washington, D.C., have distances calculated from it.

46. The neighborhood of NoMa in Washington, D.C., was once known as Swampoodle.

47. The Old Post Office, located at 1100 Pennsylvania Avenue, is the second-tallest building in Washington, D.C., at 315 feet (96 meters) tall. The Basilica of the National Shrine of the Immaculate Conception's Knights Tower is the tallest, standing 329 feet (100 meters) tall.

48. The White House has previously been known as the "President's Palace," the "Executive Mansion," and the "President's House."

49. The district's residents were only granted the right to vote for president in 1961 with the 23rd Amendment.

50. John Adams became the first president to live in the White House when the president and his wife, Abigail, moved in in 1800.

UNITED STATES
TERRITORIES

1. The United States has five inhabited territories, which are sub-national administrative divisions. Puerto Rico, American Samoa, Guam, the United States Virgin Islands, and the Northern Mariana Islands are all overseen by the United States federal government.

2. Baker Island, Howland Island, Jarvis Island, Johnston Atoll, Kingman Reef, Midway Atoll, Navassa Island, Palmyra Atoll, and Wake Island are uninhabited territories of the United States.

3. Bajo Nuevo Bank is an uninhabited reef involved in a sovereignty dispute between Colombia, Honduras, and the United States.

4. Serranilla Bank, a partially submerged reef and uninhabited islets, is the subject of a sovereignty dispute between Colombia, Nicaragua, and the United States.

5. Puerto Rico is the most populous territory of the United States, with a population of 3,285,874. There are 20 states and Washington, D.C., with a population smaller than that of Puerto Rico.

6. Puerto Rico is home to El Yunque, the only tropical rainforest in the U.S. National Forest System.

7. Puerto Rico is in the Caribbean Sea, east of the Dominican Republic and west of the U.S. Virgin Islands.

8. Puerto Rico is often called the "Island of Enchantment."

9. The capital city of Puerto Rico is San Juan.

10. Puerto Rico has two official languages, Spanish and English.

11. Puerto Rico officially became a United States Territory in 1917.

12. The Taino people were the indigenous inhabitants of Puerto Rico before the arrival of Christopher Columbus.

13. The Arecibo Observatory, known for its massive radio telescope, was featured in movies like *Contact* and *GoldenEye*. The telescope collapsed on December 1, 2020, and as of 2023, there is no plan to rebuild or replace it.

14. Ponce de Leon, a Spanish explorer, was the first to establish a European colony on the island. On August 8, 1508, Caparra was founded.

15. The San Juan National Historic Site includes the oldest European structures in the U.S. National Park Service.

16. La Casa Blanca, now a house museum, is the oldest continuously inhabited residence in the Western Hemisphere, having been built in 1521.

17. Puerto Rico has its own Olympic team and competes separately from the United States in the Olympics.

The Big Book of State Facts

18. La Fortaleza in San Juan is the oldest executive mansion still in use in the Western Hemisphere, having been completed in 1540.

19. The capital city of Guam is Hagåtña (/hə'gɑːtnjə/) (formerly known as Agana (/ə'gɑːnjə/)).

20. Chamorro and English are the official languages of Guam.

21. Guam is often called "Where America's Day Begins" due to its location near the International Date Line.

22. Guam is the largest island in Micronesia.

23. The Latte Stone, a distinctive stone pillar used in ancient Chamorro construction, is a symbol of the island's heritage.

24. Guam is home to Andersen Air Force Base, a major U.S. military installation in the Pacific.

25. Guam's highest point is Mount Lamlam, which is 1,332 feet (406 meters) above sea level. Mount Lamlam's peak is believed to be the most significant change in elevation over a short distance in the world.

26. Guam is home to the War in the Pacific National Historical Park, established in 1978 to commemorate the battles of World War II that occurred in the Pacific Ocean theater.

27. Ferdinand Magellan was the first European to arrive in Guam. The Portuguese navigator, sailing for the King of Spain, arrived sighted the island on March 6, 1521.

28. Guam is part of the "Ring of Fire," an area in the Pacific Ocean known for seismic activity and volcanic eruptions.

29. The Mariana Trench, the deepest ocean trench reaching depths of over 35,000 feet (10,668 meters), is located just east of Guam.

30. Guam's Fort Nuestra Señora de la Soledad is a historic fort built during Spanish colonial rule dating back to between 1802 and 1819.

31. Guam officially became a territory of the United States in 1898.

32. The U.S. Virgin Islands is a group of islands located in the Caribbean Sea, including St. Croix, St. Thomas, and St. John.

33. The U.S. Virgin Islands are made up of over 50 total islands.

34. The capital city of the U.S. Virgin Islands is Charlotte Amalie, located on St. Thomas.

35. English is the official language of the U.S. Virgin Islands. French, French Creole and Virgin Islands Creole English are also commonly spoken.

36. The indigenous Ciboney and Arawak peoples initially inhabited the U.S. Virgin Islands.

37. Christopher Columbus explored the islands during his second voyage to the Americas in 1493. Columbus is believed to be the first European to see the islands.

38. The U.S. Virgin Islands were purchased by the United States from Denmark in 1917 for $25,000,000 (the equivalent of $597 million in 2023).

39. The Sandy Point National Wildlife Refuge on St. Croix is a nesting site for endangered leatherback sea turtles.

40. The U.S. Virgin Islands celebrate Transfer Day on March 31 to commemorate the islands' transfer from Denmark to the United States.

41. Saint Thomas is home to Fort Christian, a Dano-Norwegian fort built between 1672 and 1680.

42. The capital of American Samoa is Pago Pago.

43. English and Samoan are the official languages of American Samoa.

44. American Samoa is part of the more extensive Samoan archipelago.

45. American Samoa is comprised of Tutuila, Aunu'u, Ofu, Olosega, Ta'u, and two coral atolls, Swains and Rose Atoll.

46. Ofu and Olosega are connected by the Ofu-Olosega Bridge, which was built in 1970.

47. The *fale* is a traditional Samoan house made of thatch and wood.

48. American Samoa became a United States territory in 1900 and became self-governing in 1967.

49. The Pago Pago Harbor has the highest annual rainfall of any harbor in the world and is one of the largest natural harbors in the world.

50. The capital of the Northern Mariana Islands is Saipan.

51. The official languages of the Northern Mariana Islands are English, Chamorro, and Carolinian.

52. The Northern Mariana Islands are composed of 14 islands, but only three are inhabited: Saipan, Tinian, and Rota.

53. Guam, a separate United States territory, is part of the Mariana Archipelago, which includes the Northern Mariana Islands.

54. The Northern Mariana Islands are officially the Commonwealth of the Northern Mariana Islands (CNMI).

55. The Taga House on the island of Tinian in the Northern Mariana Islands is an ancient Chamorro house with stone walls and a thatched roof.

56. The Banzai Cliff on Saipan in the Northern Mariana Islands is a historic site where many Japanese civilians jumped to their deaths during the Battle of Saipan in 1944.

57. The Northern Mariana Islands were part of the Trust Territory of the Pacific Islands under U.S. administration after WWII. The Territory of the Pacific Islands was a United Nations trust territory from 1947 to 1994.

58. Mount Tapochau, at 1,555 feet (474 meters), is the highest elevation on the island of Saipan in the Northern Mariana Islands.

59. The Northern Mariana Islands officially left the Trust Territory of the Pacific Islands on December 22, 1990, with governmental control being undertaken by the United States government from that date forward.

60. All inhabited Territories of the United States recognize the United States Dollar (USD) as the primary form of currency.

EVEN MORE FACTS

1. Square dancing is the official state dance of 24 different states.

2. Milk is the official state beverage of 20 states.

3. The European honey bee is the official state insect of 16 states.

4. One World Trade Center is the tallest building in the United States, standing 1,776 feet (541 meters) tall. The height was chosen to symbolize the year the United States Declaration of Independence was signed.

5. Riverside Church in New York City is the tallest church in the United States and the 25th tallest church in the world.

6. The largest orchid collection in the United States can be found at Huntington Botanical Gardens in San Marino, California—the gardens house over 10,000 orchid plants.

7. Gettysburg National Cemetery in Gettysburg, Pennsylvania, along with Arlington National Cemetery in Arlington, Virginia, make up the two cemeteries in the United States National Cemetery System.

8. Nevada is the most mountainous state in the country, with over 300 named ranges and over 100 unnamed ranges.

9. On August 25, 2023, Virginia's Fort A.P. Hill was officially renamed Fort Walker, making it the only United States Army installation named solely after a woman. Dr. Mary E. Walker is known for having treated wounded Union soldiers throughout the Civil War.

10. The Rough Riders Hotel in Medora, North Dakota, is the oldest hotel in the state, having been built in 1884. The hotel's dining room is named after President Theodore.

11. The town of Ruso, North Dakota, tripled in population from 2022 to 2023. Three people now call the town of Ruso home.

12. The United States Marine Corps War Memorial, also known as the Iwo Jima Memorial, is located near Arlington National Cemetery in Arlington County, Virginia.

13. The United States Marshals Service is the oldest federal law enforcement agency in the United States. The agency was founded in 1789.

14. New River Gorge National Park in West Virginia is the newest national park, being granted the title in 2020.

15. The United States is home to 63 national parks.

16. Eight United States presidents have come from Virginia (William Henry Harrison was born in Virginia but was a resident of Ohio when elected), seven have come from Ohio, five have come from New York, and four have come from Massachusetts. No other state has had more than two.

17. Eleven vice presidents of the United States have come from New York, six have come from Indiana, four have come from Massachusetts, and three have come from Kansas and Texas. All other states are home to two or fewer.

18. Eight presidents of the United States have died while in office. Abraham Lincoln, James A. Garfield, William McKinley, and John F. Kennedy were assassinated.

19. Six of the top 10 most heavily guarded places in the world are in the United States—Area 51 in the Nevada desert, Fort Knox in Fort Knox, Kentucky, The White House in Washington, D.C., the Federal Reserve Bank of New York in New York City, Granite Mountain Records Vault in Little Cottonwood Canyon, Utah, and the Cheyenne Mountain Complex in Colorado Springs, Colorado.

20. Pennsylvania has more covered bridges than any other state, with 227.

21. The Chugach State Park in Anchorage is the largest urban park in the United States and the largest park in the world that is contained within a metropolitan area. The Chugach State Park is over 495,199 acres (2,004 square kilometers).

22. Sixteen cities in the United States begin with the letter "Z": Zionsville, Indiana; Zanesville, Ohio; Zion, Illinois; Zachary, Louisiana; Zephyrhills, Florida; Zebulon, North Carolina; Zimmerman, Minnesota; Zeeland, Michigan; Zumbrota, Minnesota; Zelienople, Pennsylvania; Zillah, Washington; Zolfo Springs, Florida; Zwolle, Louisianna; Zilwaukee, Michigan; Zeigler, Illinois; and Zebulon, Georgia.

Made in United States
North Haven, CT
30 January 2025

65188275R00157